GLOSSARY

TERMINOLOGY

Aerial An explosive manoeuvre where the bodyboarder launches himself into the air off the top of the wave.

Barrel A tubular section of a wave within which a bodyboarder can find the meaning of life.

Backhand To ride with your back to the wave.

Backflip An acrobatic move, a variation on an ARS.

Beachbreak Waves that break over a sandy bottom, ideal for beginners.

Booger Slang for a bodyboarder.

Bottom turn Having dropped down the face of the wave, this is the first turn a bodyboarder uses to set up his next move.

Closeout A wave which breaks along its length all at once, without peeling. Also known as a straight-hander.

CARVE A cool surf mag. Also a powerful turn that throws up loads of spray.

Cutback A manoeuvre performed on the shoulder of the wave that turns the bodyboarder back toward the pocket.

Duckdive The method used by a bodyboarder to push his or her board under an oncoming wave while paddling out.

Drop in When a bodyboarder/surfer takes off on a wave that someone else is already riding – a serious breach of surfing etiquette. Remember: the rider nearest the curl has right of way.

Ding A hole in your board. Often the result of dropping in!

Drop-knee Half-kneeling, half-standing stance.

Forehand To ride facing the wave.

Floater A manoeuvre where the bodyboarder rides over the breaking section of the wave and free-falls down the wave's curtain.

Filthy Extremely good.

Flowrider Artificial wave found at water parks.

Glassy Clean, smooth surf conditions when there is no wind.

Gnarly An evil mutha of a wave, intent on destruction – evil conditions.

Goofyfoot A drop-knee who rides right foot forward.

Going off! When the waves are really good, or someone's ripping.

Grommet A young bodyboarder with no respect for his elders, usually in need of some severe discipline.

Groundswell A swell caused by a low pressure system quite a way offshore.

High Pressure Take your towel to the beach, not your board.

Impact zone The area where the waves break.

Jack Up This describes the way a wave gathers water and elevates as it moves suddenly from deep into shallow water.

Kook An idiot who has no idea what he's doing.

Lefthander A wave that breaks left (as seen from the line-up).

Lineup The area where waves jack up before they break, where surfers wait.

Local Someone who surfs a spot regularly, and enjoys moaning on and on about crowds.

Natural foot A drop-kneer who rides left foot forward.

Nailed To get hammered by the lip of a big wave.

Offshore When the wind blows from the land to the sea, holding up the waves. The ideal wind for surfing.

Onshore The exact opposite. Time to head down the pub!

Over the falls The worst kind of wipeout, when you get dragged down and stuck in the lip of the wave.

Pit A hollow, jacking section of a wave. Pull in!

Pointbreak A rock headland around which waves peel, either to the left or right.

Pumping When the surf is going off. Head for the beach!

Pocket The part of the wave just in front of the curl, where it's steepest.

Quiver A selection of surfboards to suit different conditions.

Rails The edges of a bodyboard.

Reefbreak A wave that breaks out to sea, over a slab of rock or coral. Not suitable for beginners.

Rip A dangerous current that can pull you out to sea. If you get caught in one, don't panic, but paddle across it to where the waves are breaking.

Righthander A wave that breaks towards the right, as seen from the line-up.

Set A group of larger waves which come in periodically.

Shorebreak Where waves break close to the sand at a steep beach.

Shoulder The sloping unbroken part of the wave ahead of the pocket.

Sneaker set (also known as outside or clean up set) On bigger days the occasional set that will come through is much bigger and will 'clean up' the line-up, catching everybody unawares.

Sponger Slang for a bodyboarder.

Soup The whitewater where a wave has just broken. Also a nice hot liquid to be consumed in large quantities after a winter session.

ThreeSixty Top bodyboarding magazine and spinning manoeuvre.

Trimming Cruisin' along the green face of a wave.

Tube The same as a barrel.

Zoo A badly crowded line-up.

SECRET SPOT PERFECTION IN THE CANARY ISLANDS.

A place to defrost and regain sanity during the deepest darkest parts of winter, a place to experience waves with more power and variety than anywhere in the world and a place to party hard with the throngs of Euro tourists or to chill in isolation on an island with no cars, just you, the surf and a lot of lava. With the final event of the IBA world tour being held each year at Confital on Gran Canaria the opportunity to see the best bodyboarders in the world take on some of Europe's best waves is also a great draw.

MEXICO

Mexico has over 6000 miles of coastline, with over 1500 miles facing the Pacific. The coast is covered with beaches, points, reefs and rivermouths.

Waves vary from slow rollers to crashing barrels, and it seems that every few miles of waterfront offers a new surf spot - most of which are empty.

There is a reason for Mexico featuring so heavily in international bodyboarding publications: it is bodyboarding nirvana, and a major world bodyboarding hot spot. The beach breaks are unrivalled and the temperatures tropical.

Puerto Escondido. Blessed with one of the most perfect and powerful beach breaks on the planet, Playa Ziccatela, it combines bath like warm water with prevailing morning offshore winds which sculpt Pacific swells into the perfect bodyboarding playground. The waves tend to be best early in the mornings before the sea breeze kicks in, and then again in the evening when the wind drops for the sunset session. Add to this beachfront bars and a nightlife that has legendary status within the surfing world and you can why you might want to put Mexico top of the list for your next trip...

Check out RobBarber.com for winter coaching holidays.

PUERTO ESCONDIDO - MEXICO'S PREMIERE BODYBOARDING SPOT.

TRAVEL TIPS

The journey to the perfect wave can be a long and treacherous event. Demons bent on shattering you dreams disguise themselves as airport check in clerks, baggage handlers, mad taxi drivers and hire car agents. Their job is to try and prevent you getting to your destination with board intact and enough cash to survive. But with a few cunning tricks you can make life much less stressful.

Packing

• Protection is everything. Buy a good board bag that can hold your boards easily. It'll last for ever.
• Always carry a decent spare leash, wax and spare fins.
• Take a spare board! If you want to surf big waves on your travels make sure you've got a board that you're confident with and can handle the additional power. There is no substitute for the confidence you get from being happy with your equipment when you are paddling for the wave of your life!

Checking in

• Always be polite to the check-in folk as they have the ability to make your life hell.
• When checking boards in at the airport always ask if they are going as part of your luggage allowance because they're so light.
• If you have to weigh them put your foot under the back of the boardbag to support it and take off some of the weight.
• Most airline companies in the UK have cottoned on to the fact that they can make a bit of extra cash from surfers carrying boards and will charge you through Service Air. Always check the cost before you book your ticket. Remember the golden rule one board bag = one board.
• Make sure you budget for the board taxes.
• If you suspect your board to be damaged when you arrive at the airport after a flight check it immediately and report any damage to the representatives. Most airlines require that you sign an indemnity form these days, but that shouldn't exclude them from negligent damage.

• Always dress well when travelling. You never know when you may get an upgrade on a flight, or need to look well-presented to impress the local constabulary in places like Indonesia.

St Augustine once said, "The world is a book and those who don't travel are reading one page". To travel is to enrich your existence, to open your mind to ways of life far removed from your own, to put your problems in to perspective and to make you appreciate the world outside your little bubble. Amidst everything you experience when you travel - from the colourful cultures and traditions of distant lands to the flamboyant food and people - the one thing that really gets the heart pounding is the search for waves. Pretty much all spots are less than 24 hours away so there are no excuses: it only stays a dream if you let it.

Plus, the best and most enjoyable way to improve as a bodyboarder is to travel to new wave environments. You'll enrich your wave knowledge much quicker by sampling as many different types as possible: perfectly tapering Indonesian reefs, fast breaking Moroccan wedges, the thumping power of Canarian slabs or the wide barrels of Mexican shorebreaks are just a few great ways to broaden your horizons.

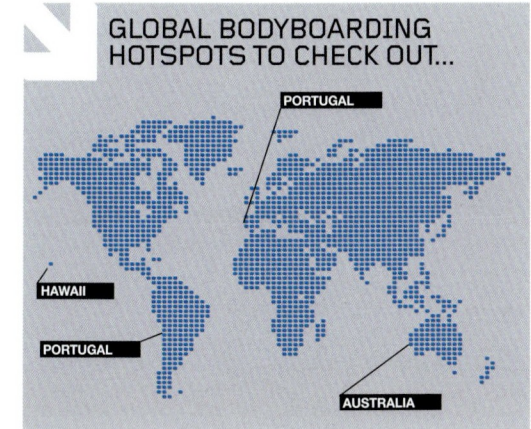

GLOBAL BODYBOARDING HOTSPOTS TO CHECK OUT...

PORTUGAL
HAWAII
PORTUGAL
AUSTRALIA

MOROCCO

Only a four hour flight from the UK, the Moroccan coast offers a vast array of points, reefs, wedges and shorebreak with stacks of undiscovered waves amongst its miles of unexplored coastline. Taghazoute in the south boasts the epic Anchor Point and is

bang in the middle of the action. The selection of waves is incredible and for the quality of the surf the crowds are still pretty low away from the main spots.

Even though Morocco is on our doorstep, it is culturally and weather-wise worlds apart! Being so close to one of the largest deserts in the world has its advantages – hot and dry winter weather conditions being one, and no wind and constant swells from the North Atlantic being a notable other. Add them together and you'll get the perfect winter surf and adventure destination. Water temperature is a comfortable 16° - 18° and the air temperature 18° - 30°. In winter....

INDO

The world renowned waves of Indonesia are the top of most experienced bodyboarder's lists.

Bali is usually the entry point to your Indonesian adventure and you'll soon appreciate that it's known as the island of the gods for good reason. Each coast is blessed with perfect reef and beach set-ups, the water is the same temperature as a bath, and the equatorial sun bakes the place for 10 months of the year. Nice.

The 18,508 known islands include such perfect wave havens as Sumatra, Java, Bali, Lombok, Nusa Lembongan and Sumbawa. It's a melting pot of religions and culture, and a dream destination for bodyboarders of all abilities.

CANARY ISLANDS

For a massive percentage of British bodyboarders the Canaries will have shaped not only their riding, but also their attitude to the sport at one point or another. Whether it's flicking a mag open and seeing some of the insane discoveries that Mickey Smith has made over there, or feeling the buzz of stepping off the plane on to a baking runway with a warm breeze on your back, having left a frosty February in the UK only three and a half hours earlier. The Canaries are the UK bodyboarder's winter saviour. They are to us what Indo is to the Aussies.

EMPTY BARRELS AT THE SUMATRAN PIPELINE, INDONESIA.

LOCATIONS

INTERNATIONAL

IMOUSANE, ONE OF MOROCCO'S MANY SICK SET UPS.

01202 433544

BOURNEMOUTH SURFING CENTRE

20 years of bodyboarding experience

Call us first for expert advice

Boards, fins, bags, leashes, accessories

www.bournemouthsurfing.com

SOUTH COAST

The south coast has a good variety of waves, with good beachbreaks at Bournemouth and Compton and a few decent reefs, both natural and manmade...There is rarely a crowd at most of the spots but Bournemouth can get hectic at weekends. If you want to have a good surf without the crowds of Cornwall, or feel like surfing somewhere different, then this is the place. Check the reports first though as these spots don't work that often and it's very likely to be flat!

PERFECT LINES AT BOURNEMOUTH.

BODYBOARDING HOT SPOTS:

Dorset – The main spots in Bournemouth are Bournemouth Pier and Boscombe Pier. These popular south-facing beachbreaks work on all tides and are usually crowded whenever there's surf. Further up the coast Southbourne is a south-facing beachbreak that works on all tides, and Highcliffe is an average south-facing beachbreak which works on low to mid. Kimmeridge Bay is a south-facing bay with shelving rock ledges. It's only really good on a southwest groundswell, with glassy conditions or light northerlies. The two main spots surfed at Kimmeridge are both best from mid to three-quarters-tide. Broad Bench (at the western end of the bay) is a shallow left and right reef-point (for advanced surfers only) which will hold waves to eight feet. When it's on it offers fast hollow waves - but expect it to be crowded. The big problem with Broad Bench is that it's part of an MoD tank firing-range, and is strictly off-limits most weekdays.

Boscombe Reef – The first Artificial Surf Reef in the Northern Hemisphere, the Reef at Boscombe (Weights Reef) was designed as a long right hander with a short sharp right. However, due to some minor technical problems, it has turned into the best Bodyboarding wave on the South Coast. A wedging peak forms left and right hand barrels and sucks dry towards low tide – boogers paradise and shortboard hell!

Best on mid tide, dangerous on low. Getting crowded, but has the advantage of dry hair walk back to the peak across the soft, sandy reef!

Isle of Wight – Striking out further into the Channel, the beaches of the Isle of Wight tend to pick up a little more swell than their neighbours on the south coast. Freshwater Bay holds a good right-hand point situated towards the western end of the island. Compton Bay is probably the most consistent spot on the Isle of Wight – it's a southwest-facing beachbreak which is best around three-quarters tide. Niton is another south-facing spot situated on the southern tip of the island which can occasionally offer good rights breaking over sand and rocks.

Hampshire and West Sussex – West Wittering and East Wittering have long stretches of southwest-facing sand and shingle beachbreak with numerous groynes. Best on southwest groundswells (which somehow wrap right around the Isle of Wight) when northerly winds blow offshore and best around high tide.

East Sussex – Brighton is a bustling seaside town with two main spots which are generally surfed on southwest windswells during the autumn and winter months. On a big swell, better quality waves break over the chalk and flint reef at The Marina which works best around mid-tide. It can get pretty crowded so is reserved for experienced bodyboarders only. Hastings has a south-facing shingle beachbreak with a wedgy shorebreak wave next to the breakwater at the Sealife Centre. There's also a small right pointbreak at Fairlight which needs a big southwest windswell to work.

Kent – Kent usually gets waves when large storms blow swell down the North Sea or up the Channel. Greatstone-on-Sea is an east-facing beachbreak which occasionally offers hollow waves at high tide on a big southwest windswell. Ramsgate is a southeast-facing beach with a couple of spots (the Harbour Wall and the Boulder Break) that occasionally work on big southwest windswells coming up the Channel. Joss Bay is another popular northeast facing spot which works on east or northeast swells. It's mostly beachbreak but there's also an area of chalk reef.

SCOTLAND

FREEZING TEMPERATURES AND COOKING WAVES CAN BE FOUND IN SCOTLAND.

The best thing about Scotland is that there is lots of it! Lots of space, fresh air, empty coastline and, most importantly, lots of swell. The Western Isles receive more swell than anywhere else in Britain and have mile after mile of beaches, reefs and points – which are empty 90% percent of the time. Scotland also has its own North Shore which runs from Thurso to Durness and is home to many world-famous spots and some hidden gems. The Northern Isles are a surf explorer's dream, with yet more waves and deserted beaches. The east coast swells are more fickle and a little more crowded, but there are probably more surfers at Fistral on a summer's day than there are in the whole of Scotland! – *Iain Masson*

BODYBOARDING HOT SPOTS:

Fraserburgh is the main surf town in the Aberdeen area. It's a northeast-facing bay with two main spots. The Broch is a beachbreak which works as a left point on biggish swells from mid to high tide. Philorth, to the east, picks up more swell and works under the same conditions while down to the south east coast, Cruden Bay is an east-facing beachbreak which works on southeast (and big north) swells. It's best from mid to high tide.

Just north of Aberdeen, Balmedie is a long stretch of southeast-facing beachbreak that works on all tides. In Aberdeen itself two spots are surfed. The Beach is a long east-facing stretch of beachbreak with numerous groynes, it works on all tides but is best on a clean south swell around low tide. Nigg Bay, just south of the city, has a boulder reef which can offer good rights on a big north swell and is best from low to mid-tide. Further south still is Lunan Bay, an east-facing beachbreak that works on all tides.

Thurso – The main town on the north coast, Thurso has two great waves. The Harbour Reef is a north-facing reef with rights and lefts that needs a biggish swell to break and works on all tides. Then of course there's one of Britain's best waves: Thurso East. This northwest-facing right reefbreak is situated a mile east of the town, opposite the castle. It is an excellent tubing wave when it's on and holds waves up to 15 feet. It's generally best from low to mid-tide, but is also good towards high tide when it's big. With fast heavy waves breaking over shallow rocks it's another break for intermediate to experts only.

Brimms Ness ('surf point' in Nordic) has a cluster of three north-facing reefbreaks situated three miles west of Thurso. A remote, exposed spot, Brimms picks up any swell going, but is badly affected by any winds other than from the south quadrant. The Bowl and The Cove are hollow righthanders which work from mid to high tide. The Point is a low tide left which wraps around the rocks at the eastern end. These are heavy waves that break over shallow rock ledges and are for experts only. Have a look around for the newly discovered breaks: Bagpipes and The Dump. They are the best bodyboarding spots in the area.

NORTH EAST

As well as being the site of numerous Nordic invasions, the northern-most limit of the entire Roman empire, the home of Lindisfarne, Sting, Dire Straits and Newcastle Brown Ale, the North East also has some of the finest waves in Britain, nay Europe! Before unleashing torrents of ridicule and slander at such a statement, it may be in your interest to try to sample some of the northern delights for yourself... Keep an eye on tight low pressure systems drifting northeast over the top of Scotland, sending waves and offshores down the North Sea.

HOME TO MOST OF THE UK'S BEST REEF SET UPS, THE NORTH EASTERN REGIONS OF ENGLAND.

ROWAN INGLES TAKES A CHOCOLATE TUBE IN THE NORTH SEA.

BODYBOARDING HOT SPOTS:

Admittedly, Newcastle isn't the first city that would spring to mind as a surf Mecca. However, with a good university, amazing nightlife and a whole stack of quality waves within an easy drive, it's not a bad place to spend some time. Bamburgh is a northeast-facing beachbreak which works on all tides. With clean water, uncrowded waves and great scenery it's a nice spot, although experienced surfers might want to do a bit of exploring around Seahouses and Beadnell to the south. The next most popular beach is at Blyth where there is a sheltered east-facing beachbreak adjacent to south wall of the harbour. It needs a big swell to work and is best from mid to hightide.

Scarborough is a seaside town which, with loads of B+Bs, a good nightlife and breaks either side of the headland, has become one of the East coast's most popular surf towns. The North Bay faces north and offers waves breaking over sand and rocks. It works from low to mid-tide with a sick high tide shorey called Supasucks. South Bay is an east-facing beachbreak that needs a big swell to work: it's best from low to mid-tide and is suitable for beginners too.

Cayton Bay – Just down the coast, Cayton Bay is a popular northeast-facing bay with three main spots. Osgodby Point at the northern end is a gnarly left reef-point which works on big north swells at high tide. The Pumphouse, inside the Point, is a mid to high-tide spot with waves breaking over sand and rocks. Bunkers, at the southern end, is a beachbreak which is best from mid to high-tide. All breaks can be classic on their day. On the right conditions some of the best waves in the UK can be found on the North East reefs.

WALES

Wales has a lot to offer bodyboarders, with a wide variety of breaks from gentle beaches to gnarly reefs. The biggest and best waves come alive during the winter months, when gales blow and lots of sheltered points and bays really turn on. Some real talent has emerged from such places as Llantwit Major, Porthcawl, Gower and more recently Pembrokeshire. Turn up at any of these spots on good days and you will see some excellent surfing. There are still a few semi-secret spots throughout Wales, but due to massive tidal movements, fickle winds your finger has to be on the pulse if you're to score them. The water in winter can also get down to seven degrees, which with a howling wind-chill calls for some serious commitment.

BODYBOARDING HOT SPOTS:

Porthcawl – needs a fairly large south westerly swell to work. The point needs a big swell to break and northerly winds to make it glassy. It holds up to 6 foot and is best at mid to high tide.

Aberavon – a wedgy peak that breaks over a sand bottom, the main break is situated next to the breakwater at the southern end of the beach.

The Gower – A selection of bays and reefs that need to be explored.

Hells Mouth (Porth Neigwl) – is a four mile long bay in north Wales. Best at high tide it offers one of the best lefthand wedges in the country when it's on.

ONE OF WALES HIDDEN TREASURES.

CHANNEL ISLANDS

Jersey and Guernsey have something to offer all standards of surfers, from gnarly big-wave reefs to protected coves with gentle surf.

On small swells head to the westerly facing beaches. St Ouen's on Jersey has a variety of spots from long walls to snappy sandbars. These spots will also hold waves up to eight feet when it's clean. If you aren't into big waves then you can find clean smaller surf at St Brelade's, which can produce fun lefts and rights on its day. On a good day at The Splash or Secrets, you may find it hard to get a wave as the locals have got it wired and the longboarders, as with everywhere in the world, are greedy!

The Channel Islands, situated 15 miles from France's Cherbourg peninsula, receive the same west swells as Cornwall and Devon. With a tidal range of up to 40 feet, continuously shifting peaks and rip currents affect many of the breaks.

There is a bodyboard club on the island called the Jersey Bodyboarders, which was formed in 2004 to promote the sport in the island, and to organise contests in waves more suited to bodyboarding. Today the club runs a variety of events in different types of waves throughout the year, and new members and visitors are always welcomed to take part. The club also organises social events and charity bodyboard events.

The club is always available to offer advice on bodyboarding / or local conditions, and can be contacted via admin@jerseybodyboarding.com or call 01534 747703. More information can be found at the club's website www.jerseybodyboarding.com

BODYBOARDING HOT SPOTS:

Greve De Lecq – a small north facing bay on Jersey that needs a huge swell to work and is best around low tide.

Water splash – the most popular break on Jersey is best at low tide. It gets more swell than most places but can get super crowded.

Vazon Bay – is a northwest facing bay with an area of beachbreak (best from low to three-quarters tide) towards the northern end, and a central rocky area - Vazon Reef - with a left breaking off either side.

PERFECT JERSEY PEAK AT SUNSET.

ORCA SURF
THE ONLINE SURFSHOP

WWW.ORCASHOP.CO.UK
MAIL ORDER HOTLINE: 01637 878074

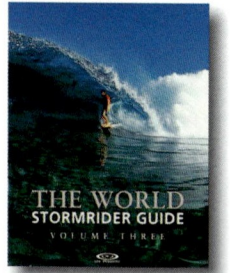

CORNWALL

PORTHTOWAN GOING OFF.

NORTH CORNWALL

Widemouth Bay in Bude a popular west facing beachbreak that works best from quarter-tide up, with waves often improving towards high tide.

Tolcarne Wedge, Newquay – probably the most well known bodyboarding wave in Cornwall. At high tide the wedging shorebreak offers massive ramps but, as a result, does get very crowded.

Portreath – The harbour wall and its suck rock take off offer a high performance wave that has honed the skills of many of the country's top riders including Prisk, Jago, Hawke and Catten. At high tide when the banks are right the Vortex offers an excellent wedging shorebreak.

Porthtowan is a north facing beachbreak which works on all tides: one of the few beaches in the area which is good around high tide. There are strong rips when over three foot, and it can get crowded when it's on.

SOUTH CORNWALL

Porthleven holds an excellent righthand reefbreak, situated just west of the town's harbour entrance. It's widely regarded as the country's best wave and, if you are ever lucky enough to see it breaking, you'll see why. The breeding ground for Mickey Smith, Jack Johns and Rohan Inglis. There are more waves in this area, so have a look around.

Praa Sands is a southwest facing beachbreak which works on southwest swells, best from mid to three-quarters tide.

DEVON

SOUTH DEVON

Bantham – a south west facing beachbreak at the mouth of the River Avon. It can offer excellent fast rights in the rivermouth when it's on, and good rights by the rocks at the southern end of the bay.

Challaborough is on the other side of Burgh Island sand spit. It offers more protection from adverse winds and can often offer good wedgy booger friendly peaks when it is onshore.

Wembury is a south-facing spot with waves breaking over sand and rocks. Best from low to mid tide.

NORTH DEVON

Croyde – North Devon's most popular beachbreak is one of the hollowest breaks on the Atlantic coast. Facing west it picks up most swell and offers excellent tubing, rampy waves at low tide with easterly winds.

Lynemouth – is a lefthand pointbreak which reels off over a cobblestone bottom at the mouth of the river Lyn. It only works during huge swells and usually gets super crowded.

OLLIE MEDLAND DROP KNEES THROUGH A HOLLOW CROYDE SECTION.

IRELAND

The west coast of Ireland has a lot going for it. Epic reef breaks and a consistently swell pounded coast, with waves to suit every ability. From miles of gentle beachbreaks for beginners, to world-class reef and pointbreaks for the advanced bodyboarder.

The water is cold, especially in the winter, and the conditions you have to contend with can be bitter. Gales and hailstones in February can put off even the hardiest surfers! Autumn is the best season, when North Atlantic low-pressure systems are at their most active and the prevailing winds are offshore. This combination can produce waves to rival those of Hawaii or Indonesia. The northwest is a major tourist centre with a variety of accommodation, entertainment to suit all wallet sizes and endless potential for flat day fun. Local bodyboarders are hardcore but laid back and friendly. Showing respect to the local surfers goes a long way and will ensure that you leave as a friend... Bain taitneamh as na tonnta! (Enjoy the waves!)

ONE OF MANY NEWLY DISCOVERED REEFS, THE BUMBALOID BARES ITS TEETH.

TOM GILLESPIE DROPPING IN TO A MUTANT RILEY'S KEG.

Through the early noughties Ireland has gained international recognition as one of the best bodyboarding spots in the world. Mickey Smith, Jack Johns and their crew of explorers have unearthed some of the world's best bodyboarding waves.

BODYBOARDING HOT SPOTS:

Rileys - Located in the Lahinch area, this slabbing lefthander offers a flat bottomed barrel and holds waves up to 15 feet.

Bundoran - similar to Newquay in Cornwall but way smaller, Bundoran is Ireland's surf city. The peak is probably Ireland's most famous wave. It offers a short hollow right and a long bashable left.

Tullan Strand - located just to the south of Bundoran town is Tullan Strand. A long west facing beach it picks up heaps of swell and often has a wave when everywhere else is flat. Fun wedgy peaks break next to the rocks at the southern end.

For further info on Ireland check out Bodyboard Manual online.

LOCATIONS

THE UK AND IRELAND >>

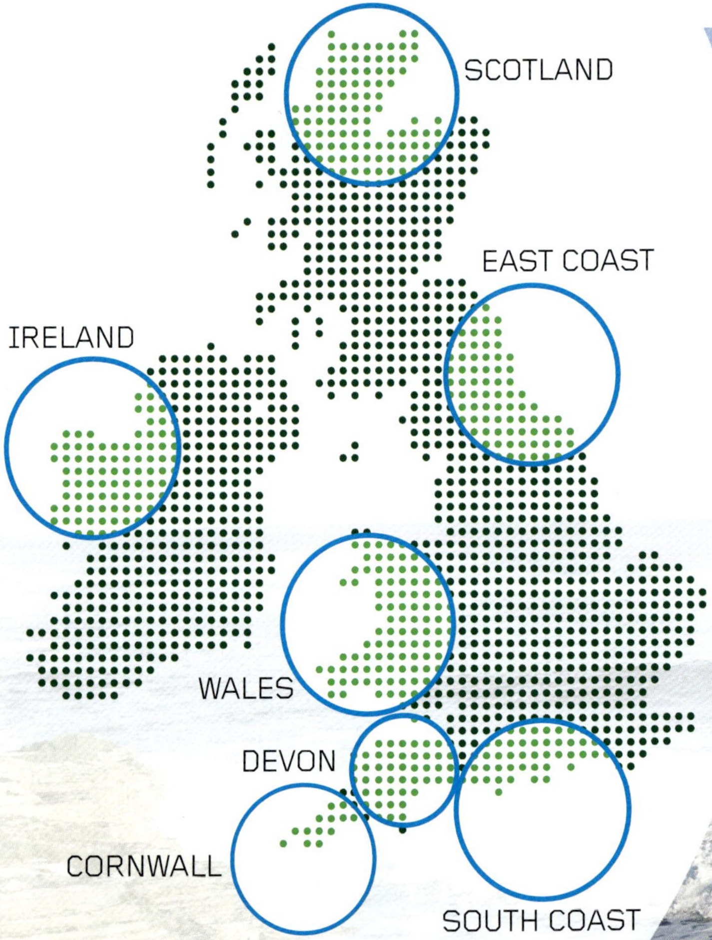

SCOTLAND

EAST COAST

IRELAND

WALES

DEVON

CORNWALL

SOUTH COAST

ONE OF SCOTLANDS SECRET SLABS.

Bodyboarding in Britain can be testing at times. With long flat spells and a mellow continental shelf, it's sometimes difficult to find waves conducive to high quality bodyboarding (or any waves at all!). On the plus side, scoring good waves becomes so much more rewarding and, with the advent of accurate surf prediction websites and weather models, it's easier than ever to get to the right spot on the right day at the right time.

In this section we check out some of the best spots in the bodyboarding hotbeds of the UK.

It's always great to score sick waves, but following the well trodden path to the breaks that appear in this manual (and on plenty of surf guide website all over the world) will lead to breaks becoming more and more crowded. The following pages offer a guide to some of the better bodyboarding areas and spots around the UK and Ireland, but don't be a sheep! Crack out the Ordinance Survery Map, take a coastal walk and unearth your own little slice of surf heaven: there are plenty still to find.

If you're still feeling the sport out and these well known spots are plenty for you at the moment, then get more information on these breaks on the beach guide on the ThreeSixty website. Go to 360mag.co.uk, there are also links to the country's best webcams.

WILL BAILEY

MOTVIATING YOURSELF TO PADDLE OUT WHEN THE WAVES ARE THIS GOOD ISN'T SUPER DIFFICULT, IT'S MORE THE ONSHORE, RAINY ONES THAT BECOME DIFFICULT TO DEAL WITH.

APRES SESSION THAW OUT.

There is no worse feeling (and no excuse for) planning to go bodyboarding, getting a crew together and then bottling it at the last minute because of the cold. You'll just regret it later, and it may be the last chance you get to surf for the next few weeks.

SHORT SHARP BURSTS
In summer we all surf for hours, but in the winter you get colder quicker which – aside from being generally unpleasant – will affect your ability to perform. Go for shorter sessions and aim to catch more waves and bust more moves. Time your session to get the best out of the tide, wind and crowd conditions. If you make sure that you've got a dry wetsuit to jump into it'll be much easier to get moving. After your session, try to hang your wetsuit somewhere warm and dry, or – worst case – leave it in a black bin-bag in the winter sun!

As soon as you get out of the car and are greeted with the cold, go for a gentle jog and stretch to warm yourself up. Then pull your suit on as quick as you can and get out there. Study the break and use channels and rips to plan the paddle out route needing the least amount of duckdives. If you're using a beach not too far from your home or where you're staying then get some decent car seat covers so that you can drive home in your wettie and get changed in the warm.

CORRECT KIT
If you've got wetsuit socks with holes in them or a wettie that lets water leak down the back, you'll dread hitting the water even more. Christmas marks the beginning of the coldest stretch of winter, so if you're a grom ask for gloves, hoods and the like from Santa. Everybody else should be able to hook stuff up in the January sales.

Having the best kit is going to help you combat (and enjoy!) the worst elements that Mo' Nature can throw at you. Check out the season's best wetties, and get the one that fits you the best. Go on: treat yourself!

BODYBOARD MANUAL 51

EXTRA TIPS

WINTER MOTIVATION

From Christmas to the end of March is a harsh time to be a bodyboarder in Britain. The water is incredibly cold, the amount of daylight that we get is limited, the amount of kit that you need is ridiculous and getting changed in freezing temperatures is a shivering nightmare.

Surfing at the weekends is often the only option, so keeping your focus and motivation can be incredibly difficult, especially if for a couple of weekends in a row the waves are slack or the wind is wrong so you don't end up getting in.

But staying motivated is key, and is all about getting yourself into a good positive mind-set for these dark times. Remember, autumn to spring is the best season in Britain for swell consistency and for offshore winds. Look on the winter as a time for boosting big moves in big waves – a chance for you to prove to yourself that you can hack it in those more powerful swells – not as a time to stagnate until next summer's trip to France. It's you against the elements – have you got what it takes?

Check out the following techniques to stay on top of your game and fend off those winter blues.

GO FOR GOALS!
Goal-setting is the easiest way to maintain drive at any sport. Bodyboarding differs slightly from the likes of football and athletics though, because most of us don't partake in it to be competitive or win anything. It's just because we enjoy the waves and the lifestyle.

Set yourself practical goals like aiming to surf at least four times a week, or advanced ones like learning to land inverts in the next four months. Having a target to achieve will increase your motivation and give you heaps of satisfaction when you achieve your goal.

GET PSYCHED!
Watch DVDs before you leave the house and focus on the moves that the guys are busting. There's no reason why you can't pull moves like the ones the guys in the those vids are doing. Sure – you've got more rubber wear on – but that's no excuse!

Getting amped to music also helps to focus your mind set and psyche you up for your next session. Some people use thrashy punk stuff whilst others find that more laid-back Moby-style stuff works for them.

Music can be that crucial bit of leverage to get you out of the car on those frosty earlies.

GLOSSARY

DROP KNEE AIRS

A LEAPING SALMON! AIDAIN GRABS HIS RAIL TO CONTROL HIS BOARD THROUGH ONE OF THE HARDEST MOVES IN BODYBOARDING, THE DROP KNEE AIR.

The frontside dropknee aerial is one of the most challenging and rewarding manoeuvres in bodyboarding. They are achievable with the right surf conditions with enough practice...

As with all things in bodyboarding the key is speed. The faster you're going the more stable you are going to be and the higher you can potentially punt.

The easiest section to launch a dropknee air off is a semi barrelling oncoming section. They are possible off closeout sections or out of the pocket, but these are much more difficult (unless your name is Dave Hubbard).

From the take off you want to do whatever is necessary to ensure that you are going to hit the pitching part of the lip with as much speed as possible. So take a mid face line, try to engage as much of your inside rail as possible and go to warp speed. The part of the wave I try to aim for is the 'corner' where the pitching part of the lip meets the open face of the wave. This is going to provide you with the best section to launch off.

As you drive towards the lip try and gauge how hard you are going to hit the section. The faster you're going the less you need to throw yourself into the manoeuvre (the wave will do more of the work for you and if you overcook it you will fly off out of control in a kind of pseudo karate kick). Conversely the slower you are moving the more effort you are going to have to throw into the move.

As you hit the lip you need to perform a few actions at the same time. Firstly un-weight your board by throwing your arms up in the air. You should simultaneously be twisting your shoulders towards the beach – this will change the direction of your travel from parallel with the wave to heading inwards. As you are in the air a good idea is to grab your wave side rail with your wave side hand (like an Indie Grab on a skate/ snowboard), this will help to hold the board under you and stabilise you through the manoeuvre (it also looks super kick ass). It's important at this point to keep your head up looking at the beach (don't get sucked into looking at your board as you go for the grab).

As you start to descend, release the rail and look to flatten your board as much as possible for the landing. This is the most difficult part of the move especially if the wave is pitching top to bottom. In which case try and position your weight so that it is more towards the back of the board as this will prevent you from nose diving. Hopefully you'll land cleanly being pushed along by the white water and just have to soak up the cries of adulation from all who witnessed your mad DK skills.

The perfect wave for attempting airs (and landing them) is a 2-4ft wedge with a light to medium cross/ offshore breeze blowing into the breaking wave. By having a wedging wave it will ensure that you have plenty of speed and (to use skateboarding terminology) your roll in is going to be bigger than your ramp, thus ensuring plenty of potential for boosting above the lip. By heading into the wind when you launch, your board will be held underneath you making it easier to control and increasing the likelihood of you stomping your move (hopefully in front legions of other wave riders who will now worship you and your aerial offensive). Good examples of frontside airs being performed can be found on *The Inside* (Paul Trevor Roach) and Bud Miyamoto on *Boogie Nation*.

USING HIS ARM TO STALL, DANNY WALL KEEPS IT CASUAL IN A PORTHLEVEN BARREL.

ROGER SHARP

DROP KNEE TUBE

Tube riding is the essence of any kind of wave riding and drop knee is no different...

When taking off on a barrelling wave dropknee, it is essential that your board is pointed straight at the beach - this will help you engage your rail with the wave face as you go into your bottom turn (Buy a copy of Fu Manchu and slow-mo Kainoa McGee's take offs at Pipe for the best possible examples of this).

As you get towards the bottom of the wave twist your shoulders and swing your arms into the direction you wish to travel. Simultaneously apply pressure to your wave side knee this will cause you to bottom turn and bring you up the face of the wave.

As the wave starts to barrel you will need to judge what kind of line you are going to pick. The hollower the wave, the lower you will need to be on it to avoid being sucked over the falls. If the wave is a pinching or a semi barrelling wave, then you may need to pick a higher line to make sure you get into the tube.

Once in the barrel straighten your back leg and your back as much possible. This will ensure that your wave side rail stays engaged in the wave face and you don't slide out (more importantly you will look way cooler than if you're hunched over or sitting on your back leg!).

To control your speed put your hand in the wave face (stick it in to slow it down pull it out to accelerate). When you are in the barrel try and focus on the top corner of it (remember where you look is where you end up, so don't watch where you are going watch where you want to go, in this case aim you're aiming for the exit).

Hopefully you have timed the wave correctly and matched your speed to how fast the wave is breaking. This will mean you get blown out of the barrel with the spit of the wave and with your mates whooping! If you want to fast track your tube riding skills I recommend spending some quality time in Bali where the waves are perfectly suited to getting barrelled...

DROP KNEE

DROP KNEE CUTBACKS

AIDAN CARVES UP A MOROCCAN SHOULDER.

FORE HAND CUTBACKS

Once you've mastered taking off and bottom turning on dropknee, the natural move to learn next will be a dropknee cutback.

Step 1
When you've ridden out of the pocket, initiate the turn by centring your weight on your board and releasing your rail edge. Lean your weight on to your front foot and gradually, smoothly, lean onto your outside rail. Apply pressure with your front foot. Turn your shoulders and head back towards the broken wave behind you.

Step 2
Some bodyboarders now choose to grab the inside rail (which confusingly becomes your outside rail as you change direction) as they lean into the turn. This can be essential if you're entering the turn at speed. As you jam the turn, push the tail of the board with your back leg but ensure that you keep the rail engaged or you'll go into a slide. Head back in the direction that you are aiming to travel with your spare arm.

Step 3
As you change direction you will be facing back into the whitewater: try to buffer off of it, so that it naturally pushes you back into the direction that you were heading originally. Now that you're back in the power pocket, put your weight back on the inside knee, refocus down the line and start eyeing the upcoming section for your next stunt.

Quick Tips
• Gain plenty of speed in small waves by pumping through a smooth bottom turn.
• Instead of jamming a short snappy turn, try to turn through an arc so that you completely change direction and get back to the wave's power pocket.
• Get your weight back onto your front foot to flatten your board and continue down the line.

A SWOOPING BACKHAND CUTBACK.

BACK HAND CUTBACKS

The backside carve is one of my favourite manoeuvres in bodyboarding. If performed properly it looks cool and will throw up enough spray to have people on the beach reaching for their umbrellas. Plus it will position you back in the bowling part of the wave.

The faster you are travelling into your cutback the more impressive it will be, so again the key is speed. Once you spot the section of the wave you want to perform your cutback on (look for a nice slopping wall) drive towards it by applying pressure to your front foot.

As you get towards the top third of the wave throw your arms and twist your shoulders towards the beach, and then back towards the breaking part of the wave. This will cause your weight to transfer from your wave side rail to your beachside rail.

As you continue through the turn try to keep tightening the arc so that by the time you have finished turning back towards the wave you are positioned mid face. This means that when you turn to face back down the line you will be in a better position to gain speed and continue your dropknee onslaught.

The mechanics of doing a backside cutback are almost identical to doing a frontside bottom turn and – as it's your knee side rail that's engaging with the wave - you can put a lot more weight into the turn allowing you to throw more spray and still maintain control.

For amazing demonstrations of backhand cutbacks check out old school footage of Joey Viera as well as more recent footage of Matt Lackey and Mason Rose who all prove that backhand dropknee is a functional and effective style of wave riding...

DROP KNEE FLOATERS

THE CLOSE OUT FLOATER.

The DK floater is an essential move for aspiring and experienced drop knee riders alike. Having mastered the takeoff and trim you should now be wondering what to do with those feathering lips!

Step 1
Head along the wave and, providing nobody's dropped in or paddled directly into your path, keep focused on a section to float. When a section of the wave in front of you is about to break it's time to begin your approach. The more speed you have the more likely you are to land it (and to look good doing so!).

Step 2
Direct your board towards the lip as it starts to feather. Each lip will require a different approach and different timing. Knowing how and when the wave will break only really comes with experience. Watching videos will help but they can't portray the perspective you will be experiencing when approaching the lip. Remember timing is crucial, so practise is the only thing that'll help you improve.

Step 3
You should now be at the weightless point on top of the lip thinking about your descent: here's where your hand comes in. On a standard floater I'll use my hand to grab the rail – keeping my board under me during the free fall – always remember to release it from the board before impact. If you are going really fast and are super-confident then you can get away with not using your hand - although I think it tends to look better with the grab.

Step 4
Positioning yourself directly over the board at all times during the move will help. If you're going as fast as you should be, it's the best place for you. Charge the lip with confidence and once you're up there don't have second thoughts about the drop. You'll be surprised what a little faith in your ability can achieve – in fact it's often the difference between the ripper and the kook!

Step 5
Move your weight forward on your board to ride out of the move, use your out stretched arms to keep your balance, then bottom turn into your next move.

BODYBOARD MANUAL 45

DROP KNEE

GETTING UP

AIDAN SALMON DEMONSTRATES A CLEAN DROP KNEE TAKE OFF.

Learning to get up dropknee is one of the most frustrating elements of bodyboarding.

Everything works against you - from the size of your board and the fact it has no fins in it, to the fact you're wearing flippers. However, dropknee is an awesome element of the sport of bodyboarding, and something that you must persevere with...

The first thing you need to do is paddle as hard and as fast as you can. If you are going to be getting up on your board then you need to be moving a lot faster than if you're riding prone. It's a bit like riding a bike: the faster you're moving the more stable you are, thus you will have a better chance of a killer ride.

The next important aspect is the angle that you paddle into the wave at: if it's a smaller fatter wave then you can get away with paddling in on a 45 degree angle which will mean you are already moving across the face by the time you get up (watch Paul Roach at Seaside on Wave Slaves, or Aka Lyman at Rocky Point circa 1994). Although if the wave's a big hollow beast, then you'll have to paddle into it pointing straight at the beach or you will slide out and eat it as soon as you get up. Good examples of this being done successfully can be seen on Fu Manchu with Kainoa McGee at Pipe or Ala Moana.

So, assuming the wave you're taking on is an average Brit beach break, you can probably take it on an angle. As you feel the wave pick you up, transfer your weight forward - this will flatten the board off by reducing drag from the tail thus increasing speed and making you more stable. Remember flat is fast.

Now, as you are being propelled along by the wave and no longer by paddle power it's time to get up. Place both hands over the nose of the board and use them to anchor your body as you draw your knees up. Your knees should only come up far enough for your ankles and fins to be protruding from the tail of you board. Once your knees are up keep your weight forward (otherwise you will lose the wave) and bring your front foot up. You can bring your foot up by bringing it straight through under your chest or by swinging it around the outside of your body and up onto your board. Your front foot needs to land in the top third of your board, close to (but not over) the beach side rail.

As your foot lands on the front of your board release your grip on the board and swing your arms in the direction you want to travel. It sometimes helps to point down the line with your beach side arm as this will serve to twist your shoulders and thus the rest of your body so you'll head down the line away from the breaking part of the wave. At this point straighten your back and wave side leg as much as possible - not only will this make you look cooler, but it will keep the rail engaged in the face of the wave and help prevent you from sliding out.

Remember to always look in the direction you want to travel, and not down at your board and - once you're up - the rest of the wave is your playground to throw tail and run amok on: enjoy!

BACK-FLIPS

The back-flip has to be one of the trickiest manoeuvres to pull off on a bodyboard. To help you to do these moves you need to focus on having the right kit, attitude, flexibility and a good section on a wave. Stretching and flexibility will improve your riding 100 percent and will keep your body feeling younger and fitter even when you're an old codger! Just look at Jeff Hubbard, the guy is a piece of elastic.

THE BACK FLIP, AS DEMONSTRATED BY BEN PLAYER IN TAHITI.

For all air manoeuvres, speed and timing is critical. With the take off lean your weight forward to maximise your speed through the bottom turn. Keep your eye on the lip of the oncoming section. You need to initiate this manoeuvre just before the lip breaks, just as it pitches.

Shot 1 Hit the lip just before it breaks, and at this point instead of twisting for an ARS (air roll spin), just lean your head back and use your weight - along with projection - to throw yourself out in front of the wave. You can practice this motion on a trampoline to get to grips with it.

Shot 2 As you leave the lip, arch your back and continue to lean your head back, tucking in your legs at the same time to clear the wave. Try to cross your legs for good style.

Shot 3 In full flight. Maintain a firm grip leaning forward and allow the nose of the board to hit the water first to cushion the landing (it can get nasty landing in the flats as you often get winded). It's now that most back-flippers will come unstuck - you must hold on tight and keep your weight centred to avoid digging the tail in.

Like all bodyboarding manoeuvres, it's desire and constant practice that will make all the difference. As you land, look in the direction you want to go and let the wave do the rest. The faster you move on landing, the more chance you have of making the move. You need to spin out of it as quickly and cleanly as possible.

As you start the move by throwing your head in the direction you want to go, finish it by throwing your head through what is effectively the final stages of a spin. Keep your legs tightly crossed to your backside for as long as you can and it will help you round.

ADVANCED

AIR ROLL SPIN (ARS)

ADAM JAGO, ONE OF THE UK'S BEST AIR ROLL SPIN EXPONANTS.

Once the most progressive move in bodyboarding, the ARS has now become a cornerstone manoeuvre of the Euro and domestic contest scene. When executed correctly it is a functional and satisfying move to land.

At the risk of stating the bloody obvious, the ARS is a combination of two manoeuvres: the air roll and forward spin. An ability to complete both these separate moves on a regular basis is a good place to start you on your way to success with this move. A wave with a decent pitching lip is required – although ARS's can be performed as the wave closes out, they almost always look better when landed back onto a clean shoulder, as Adam Jago has done in this sequence at Portreath.

Shots 1 & 2 The bottom turn is a key element in any bodyboarding manoeuvre – it provides the speed and projection required for the next step. Don't turn too far in front of the wave as you will lose speed and bog down. You can see that even at the early stage of his turn, Adam is eyeing up the section he wants to hit. It's important to watch your ramp carefully, as hitting it too early will send you off the back and too late will earn you a lip in the face. It's also interesting to note how far forward Adam is positioned on the board in the first shot, with his head level with the nose. This is to gain maximum speed, which translates into projection later on.

Shots 2 & 3 As he reaches the lip Adam tenses his body and flattens the slick of his board to the face of the wave to gain maximum projection. After launching out of the lip and beginning the air roll part of the move, keep your eyes open. If you have connected with the lip properly as it pitched you will naturally be thrown into a rolling motion. When you have gone past the apex of the roll (i.e. you are on the way down), initiate the spin by throwing your head inwards towards the face of the wave. (shot 3) You can see in the photos how Adam's back is arched and his head is looking in the direction he wants to go, forcing the rest of his body to follow: a fundamental principal of any bodyboarding manoeuvre. The speed from his bottom turn means he has projected up and out of the wave as desired.

Shots 4 & 5 Adam's board is now in a horizontal spinning position and he has crossed his legs for added style. At this point it's important to centre your body on the board and hold on tight for landing. Keep your legs lifted or you will come unstuck when you hit the wave's face again. In bigger bowly waves it's possible to complete the full spin in the air, but often you will have to complete the last part of the rotation on the face or in the whitewater. Your momentum should keep you spinning as you land and the whitewater will also help push you around if you remember to keep looking into the spin. A good tip is to try looking back around at your fins...

Shot 6 Spin completed. You might feel pretty disorientated after all that rotating, so get your bearings and, as you come back onto the shoulder, quickly re-engage your inside rail with the wave's face and get back in a trimmed position as Adam has done – enabling you to set up for your next manoeuvre. Try to resist the urge to make any outrageous claims or puff your cheeks as though you have just stared death in the face. Happy boosting!

FRONT FLIP

The front flip is a move that's been around for a long time, but not that many riders go for it – it's a bit like the double roll, the Gorf or the 'Hubb' from yesteryear.

It is a cool novelty move that's super fun to bust out in the summer though... Saffa transplant Remi Geffroy has taken the move to the extreme, boosting big flips at north coast wedges whenever he gets chance. Here's how he does it.

• You need steep, fast, punchy waves, so wedges are perfect. When there is an oncoming bowl you need to hit it early. It's similar to a Gorf - but with a flip. You need a lot of speed and aim to flip over rather than spin.

• When you hit the section you project yourself up and out of the section as far as you can to get your initial momentum and drop your inside shoulder, aiming to get your legs above your head. By twisting your board to the side it's almost like going into a forward roll.

• By pulling your legs over your head you should land forward. It's important to keep your eyes open and keep your awareness of where you are. Remi, the rider in the shot, did gymnastics for 12 years which definitely helped! If you go through the move on a trampoline it will definitely help. It also helps if you are flexible, so stretching is essential.

• The landing is straightforward. Get your board flat under your belly and the momentum of your legs should help you land projected in front of the wave. If you can boost one out of a bowl then you can land forward and carry on going. Hold on tight and go flip out!

REMI GEFFROY LAUNCHES A FORWARD FLIP.

SUN PROTECTION

SLIP, SLOP, SLAP!

If you're chilling on the beach, make sure you're wearing sun protection. And choose one that suits your skin type. Use a spray – they're a lot easier to apply than cream. In the water, use a zinc-based suncream or stick. Apply at least 20 minutes before entering the sea or it'll just drip into your eyes. Don't rub your eyes when you're wearing suncream in the sea - your eyes will sting like hell. If you don't have any suncream, try to stay out of direct sunlight as much as possible. Many a session has been ruined by suncream grease on the hands so give them a good wash then thoroughly rub them with a towel before your sesh.

ADVANCED

GYROLL

THE GYROLL, A TWEAKED VARIATION OF THE AIR ROLL SPIN.

The ideal wave to pull a gyroll has a nice bowly down-the-line section, similar to that required to execute an air roll spin. Coming out of the barrel and whacking the pitching section is the ideal scenario. The ascent towards the pitching lip must be timed correctly in order to maximise projection and therefore gyroll rotation. I would recommend that both backflips and ARS's are mastered before a gyroll is attempted as you require aspects of both these moves. Approach the lip as you would to pull a roll or an ARS. As you meet with the lip try to disengage from it using a shunting flip motion (as you would to go into a back flip). It is at this point that the move goes off on a different tangent to most others.

Slide your body across your board so that your legs and flippers hang off the side (as opposed to out the back over the tail). As shown in the photo, lean with your head and throw your weight so that you begin to almost loop back on yourself.

Shot 4. Shows the full change in direction of the board, different to that of an ARS.

Shot 3. While maintaining a tight grip on your board, try to manoeuvre your body back into the standard prone position - i.e. legs coming over the tail of the board and body positioned upon it. The landing of a gyroll is usually executed tail or rail first.

It is essential to hold on tight and try to lay the board flat to get it planing on the wave again in order to make the move. Be warned: it is not advisable to try this move in shallow shore/reefbreak waves as there is every chance that you will land on your head or back!

AIR FORWARD

If you're keen to bust the newest moves in the sport, or just looking to impress some ladies on the beach, this stunt is a classic to have tucked up your wettie sleeve.

The ideal set-up for this manoeuvre is a horse-shoeing wave with the face turning towards you, effectively giving you a ramp to hit off. Timing is crucial: hit it too late and you will get caught in the lip, too early and you will more than likely land where you started: out the back. A steep bottom turn is also needed to provide enough momentum to throw you and your board into the air.

Shot 1
Ben Player has lifted his legs and released his rail as he hits the lip. If the section is sufficient the spin can be initiated a moment before launch and will help with rotation.

Shot 2
Ben brings his body into a more central position on his board. Between shot 1 and 2, he has flicked his head in the direction he wants to spin and by arching his back has pulled himself out of the water. This has the effect of throwing his weight behind the manoeuvre and helping with rotation.

Shots 3 to 5
Ben has used his head to guide him through the move and now begins to look for a landing spot. The type of wave and projected direction will determine landing situations – on the whitewater, on the open face, or out in the flats. If you can land on the open face you're in the premier position for completion and this is what Ben is aiming to do.

Shots 5 to 7
As he comes out of the spin Ben splays his legs in an effort to slow rotation and gain control. Due to his forward momentum he is about to touch down with his rail closest to the face of the wave: this deflects much of the impact of the landing and also prevents his board from digging into the water. Once you have landed, hold on!

The hardest part of this stunt is not only the initiation of the spin, but finding a wave capable of allowing the manoeuvre to be performed and completing the spin in the air before the wave passes you by and you land off the back.

BEN PLAYER LAUNCHES A CRAZY AIR FORWARD.

ADVANCED

AIR REVERSE

JEFF HUBBARD BOOSTS THE BIGGEST AIR REVERSES OFF THE HEAVIEST SECTIONS.

Like so many of today's moves, the air reverse was pioneered by Mike Stewart, but more recently it's been taken to the next level by that aerial freak Jeff Hubbard. The first man to consistently pull the whole spin in the air demonstrates his freakish ability in this sick sequence.

Speed is more important than almost any other factor if this move is to be completed successfully – there's no faking an air reverse, especially one where you pull a complete 360 before touch-down – perhaps it's this need for speed that makes the move feel so exciting. As you can see from the sequence, Jeff Hubbard is busting this air reverse at Off The Wall in Hawaii, where gaining speed really isn't an issue. In the UK, however, you need to look for a steep, wedging wave, preferably with a horse-shoeing air section, which will give you the best possible chance of launching and landing one.

Shot 1 In the first shot Hubb has already gone through about 50 percent of the move: he's bottom-turned (milking the wave for every ounce of speed), he's eyed the spot that he wants to hit, and with impeccable timing he's initiated the first part of the move. At this point Hubb is 100 percent committed – his back is fully arched and he's looking in the direction he wants to spin.

Shot 2 The second shot shows how, due to his momentum and timing, he's been catapulted up and out of the lip. Many people in the same situation would end up doing an off-the-lip reverse, but it's Hubb's ability to 'pop it' and put vast amounts of air between him and the wave, that differentiates him from many other riders. You'll notice that his legs are crossed – making the move look more refined – and he is, after having completed half of the rotation, again looking in the direction in which he is spinning - keeping that momentum going.

Shots 3-6 Shots three and four are particularly interesting. Whereas many air reverses are half completed in the air and half completed battling with the whitewater, we can see that in this particular case Hubb's determination has seen him complete 100 percent of the rotation in the air. It's almost as if he's actively wrenched his board around mid-air to do this. The downside of this move is the landing: check how heavy it is! It is worth noting that in the fifth shot Hubb's legs are now uncrossed, helping him to stabilise his flight, and prepare for the landing by moving further down the board and start eyeing up a landing spot.

Shot 5 It's difficult to see because of the whitewater, but in the final shot you can just see how both his elbows and his body are positioned further down the board. By doing this Hubb is maximising his body's ability to absorb the impact of the landing.

HOW TO SCAM YOUR WAY TO THE BEACH BY JACOB COCKLE

THE CHEAPEST WAY TO TRAVEL – BY THUMB.

Buy an open day bus ticket and use it for the whole month!
You can do this by simply rubbing off or smudging the first part of the date. Then roll the ticket up into a small ball and use it as much as you like. The bus driver will never stamp it because it's an open day ticket. [He's joking, of course. This is illegal and you should never do it – Ed.]

Alternatively, ring your mate with transport up and tell him that the banks are amazing at whatever the tide is in the next hour: "Mate, have you seen the low tide banks, they're the best I've ever seen." Or tell him that that the wind has swung or is about to swing offshore. Or you could ask a chick who drives if she wants to go hang out on the beach or watch the sunset.

Hitchhiking. Despite its bad rep, hitching can be one of the easiest, cheapest and fastest ways of getting to the beach in summer. Tourists love surf dudes. As soon as they see your bodyboard they will know you're not going to kill them, and that you can probably help them with directions to the beach and the cheapest car park.

Camp down on the beach. That way the surf is literally in your front garden. You'll be the first in at sunrise and it doesn't cost a penny. Just be sure to clean up after yourself...

CUT BACK REVERSE SPINS

THE BIGGER THE FAN OF SPRAY CREATED THE BETTER WITH CUTBACK REVERSE SPINS.

The cutback reverse spin is one of the best ways of losing speed in a dramatic and fun style.

• Race out onto the shoulder and shift your weight from your inside rail to your outside rail as you would for a normal cutback. The best cuttie reverses begin with a really powerful cutback.
• Once you've arced through the cutback to the point that you are facing back towards the foam, you need to initiate the spin.
• The key to a good cuttie reverse is to try to kind of stop on the spot and complete the spin before riding on. This takes a lot of practice but definitely looks the best.
• Slide your weight up your board, un-weight your inside hand (so in this case my right hand) and put all your weight on your abdomen – so that you can centre yourself on your board with of all your weight in the middle.
• Throw your head over your shoulder, cross your legs up to your backside and hold on tight.
• As you come back round to the point where you are looking down the line, transfer your weight back on to your inside rail, lean forward and begin to gain speed again.

BODYBOARD MANUAL 37

ADVANCED

INVERT AIR

THE KEY TO GOOD AIRS IS TIMING. IT'S ESSENTIAL TO HIT THE LIP JUST AS THE LIP PITCHES.

Step 1
For any sort of aerial manoeuvre speed is essential. Put in a solid bottom turn and keep your board flat as you angle onto the oncoming section. The most crucial part of this step is making sure that your timing is perfect to ensure you slingshot outwards - rather than being too late and getting an embarrassing lip to the head.

Step 2
You should now be airborne and twisting your body into the invert. Your head should be completely upside down and your arms should be twisting your board inverted. Try to remember that the slower you get into this position, the more stylish it will look. Try to kick your inside leg upwards, this will split your legs and allow your body to twist upside down more easily.

Step 3
The next step is the hardest as you should now be in the invert position, where your natural reaction is to pull your board back around for landing. Instead of this you should try and pause for a fraction of a second. This will allow you to keep getting more flight as your body is still arcing through the invert...

Step 4
As you feel yourself beginning to drop down towards the wave you should begin to slowly bring your board back around yourself. If you've timed it right, the lip should hit the flats just before you do, breaking your fall.

Step 5
Throughout the landing it's essential to hold on tight. Brace your body so that you don't head-butt your board, then regain trim position as soon as possible. This will help you ride out of the move and – ideally – straight into the next!

QUICK TIPS – INVERTS
- Look for a nice ramp that is wrapping at you – wedge waves are the best to boost off.
- As you hit the lip, kick your inside leg skyward and tweak your board so that the bottom is facing upwards.
- Bring the board underneath you as you descend and hold on tight.
- Try to get back on to your rail edge as soon as you land.

TOP TIPS

- Practise edge and speed control in sucky waves to increase your technique.
- Watch videos to see how guys like Hardy and Player lunge their weight forward to increase speed and make those speedy barrels.
- Practising in closeout shorebreaks will help you become more familiar with being inside the tube. Check the explosion of the lip with the trough and then learn to negotiate the shockwaves that travel up the wave face.
- Keep your eyes open and don't dip your head – unless you absolutely need too.

ADVANCED

TUBE RIDING

Tube riding is one of the most exciting and thrilling experiences in bodyboarding. There is nothing more satisfying then pulling into an open tube and making it. In fact, tubes can become addictive. Surfers and bodyboarders travel to the four corners of the globe seeking out these sometimes perfect, sometimes frightening, but always beautiful phenomena.

In the prone position, the bodyboard is the most functional tube riding vehicle because, unlike the surfboard which is 'driven' by the feet, bodyboarders have full control with their whole body. Also we can fit into tubes that surfers would be hard pressed to squeeze into.

Tube riding is an art, and like all arts it takes time and patience to master it. You need to have the knowledge of the optimum combinations of swell, tide and wind which create the hollowest conditions at any particular break. You also need to know how to read a wave, when to stall and when to accelerate to get the maximum amount of tube time.

Step 1
This sequence of Rob Barber at a Canarian reef shows how to take off and set up for a tube. In the first shot - the take off - note how his feet are trailing in the wave which enables him to steer and control his speed. He is looking down the line to focus on what the wave is about to do.

Step 2
Shot two shows Rob in trim position after coming out of his bottom turn. He is still focusing down the line, and can see that the lip is going to pitch and barrel.

Step 3
In shots three to five he is controlling his speed to maximise tube time, and absorbing the shockwaves created by the impact of the throwing lip on the wave's trough. The deepest tube rides are a gamble of speed and control as you try to get as deep as you possibly can so that you're sat on the foam ball (at the deepest point of the tube).

Excellent edge control is essential for good tube riding as water is rushing up the wave's face at such a pace that it can become difficult to maintain your line.

Step 4
Shot six shows Rob exiting the tube with the spit – the explosion of misty water filled air that is expelled as the tube collapses – usually at the end of the ride.

ROB PLUMBS HIS WAY THROUGH A CLEAN CANARIAN BARREL.

BEN PLAYER, SHACKED IN TEAHUPOO.

QUICK TIPS – TUBE RIDE

• If you need to slow yourself down to get inside the barrel then stall by sliding your weight back on your board, sinking your legs in the water and if needs be, pull up on the nose of the board.
• As the lip envelopes you and you are inside the tube it is naturall to close your eyes as there is vapour in the air and often froth from the shock waves caused by the impacting lip. It's important to keep your eyes open and looking towards the top of the opening as this is where you are aiming for.
• Try to regulate your speed so that you achieve maximum time behind the curtain. Until you become more experienced though be aware that making the tube ride is the important thing, coming out the hole is the sign of success!
• Remember, the safest place to be on a wave is inside the tube, so once you are inside there, enjoy the view! If you fall off in side the tube then try to dive in to the trough between the impacting lip and the transition at the bottom of the wave. Then 99% of the time the wave will pass by and you'll just pop up out the back of the wave with out getting a beating.

CROWDED WAVES

WORDS: JACOB COCKLE

The best advice is to try and avoid the crowds, and the best times to catch uncrowded surf are when everyone else is at work or in bed: so sunrise, sunset, mid morning and mid afternoon.

If it is crowded then, before paddling out, examine the waves and make a mental note of where the best peaks are and how many waves are going unridden. Then look for markers on the beach so you know where to sit. Don't be afraid to leave the pack – sometimes the best waves are nowhere near where the majority of surfers are: don't be a sheep. Also, study the sandbanks and try to predict what the waves will be doing in the next few hours as the tide moves. Stretch before each surf, that way you'll be mentally and physical ready and will find it easier to get stuck in.

In the water the trick is to keep moving, picking off as many waves as possible. Try not to get sucked into waiting for the sets out back - chances are you'll be waiting a long time and there will be a lot of people fighting for them. Sometimes those small inside wedges can jack up into sick rides. Your aim should be to get as many waves as possible: more waves equals more fun!

Make sure you show respect to the locals, don't drop in or snake. Things can get nasty when the waves are overcrowded. If someone is following you around and snaking your waves then try paddling off to another peak slowly with them following, then let them get the next wave and paddle back to where the waves are good. If this doesn't work, try saying loudly: "Hasn't it got crowded in the last 10 years while I've been doing time for that murder," or, "Is that your car getting clamped in the car park?" Or, "I just got back from Indo - the doctors don't even know what it is yet," while scratching yourself with a crazed look in your eyes...

A BUSY DAY AT PORTHLEVEN.

5 BEST SPOTS TO GET BARRELLED IN THE UK AND IRELAND

RILEY'S, IRELAND   PORTHLEVEN, CORNWALL   CROYDE, NORTH DEVON   BUNDORAN PEAK, IRELAND   BAGPIPES, SCOTLAND

INTERMEDIATE

REVERSE FLOATERS AND REVERSE OFF THE LIPS

REVERSE OFF THE LIP

1
2
3

BJORN STOREY FLINGS HIMSELF IN TO AN OFF THE LIP REVERSE.

To pull a decent reverse spin off the lip of an oncoming section - or floating across a foam closeout - requires plenty of speed and good timing.

• Take off and gain plenty of down-the-line speed. Keep watching the oncoming section and position yourself in the top half of the wave so that you keep speed and can easily angle up to hit the lip and go into the move.

• As you near the pitching lip of the closeout, decide whether you are going to try to hit the lip and rebound off it so that you get some forward projection – this will mean you go into an off-the-lip reverse. If you're going to ride onto the oncoming foam and then spin into a reverse as you go across it you will be busting a reverse floater.

• Whichever you decide to do, the reverse needs to be nice and tight. So as you hit the lip or begin the floater you need to quickly slide your weight forward, throw your head over your shoulder (so in an 'out to sea' direction) and bring your legs up to your backside, keeping them nice and tight.

• With an off-the-lip reverse you should time your spin so that you hit the lip and then turn down the wave. Hopefully if you've done it correctly your tail will go up the wave, out of the top and create a fan of spray. Keep a tight grip and your legs tightly crossed during the foam explosion and you will ride victoriously out of the move.

• During a reverse floater you should hit the top of the foam and quickly throw yourself into the spin so that you actually glide across the section backwards. Ideally you will complete the whole spin before you land in the flats. Again a tight grip, tightly crossed legs and looking over your shoulder and through the turn are really important. Be careful not to dig an edge in at any point, so try not to do any jerky moves and stay centred over your board.

REVERSE FLOATER

• Once you have nailed both of these moves, air reverses are next!

32 BODYBOARD MANUAL

AIR ROLL

An air roll can be achieved on nearly any sized or shaped wave, from peeling waves to short closeouts. Its versatility means that it can be performed in a variety of situations - from hitting end sections on mushy closeouts to 'el rollo' or 'air rollo' out of the pocket on a barrelling wave.

The roll is the foundation for the more advanced off the lip manoeuvres, so it is important to get this mastered before trying anything more difficult. Here I explain how to perform a roll out of the pocket (in the barrelling section of the wave) and back onto the face of the wave

THE DOWN THE LINE AIR ROLL.

Step 1 First things first, to do a roll off the lip you must select a wave with a barrel or at least some sort of lip.

Step 2 Once you have selected a wave you'll need to think about your positioning from the moment you take off. When you first take off look down the line to see any possible sections that are going to break. Once you've spotted a possible section you need to establish where and when the wave is going to break and aim to bottom turn just behind this point.

Step 3 Lean into your bottom turn and focus on the point that you are aiming to hit. You should have moved your weight further up the board allowing you to utilise your momentum and speed to get up the face of the wave. Using your momentum achieved from the take off, you should have enough speed to reach the top of the wave and project off the pitching lip.

Step 4 If you've positioned yourself correctly and timed your bottom turn properly you should reach the lip at the critical point when it is about to pitch. As you approach the lip get a good grip of your board otherwise it will be knocked out of your hands.

When you hit the lip don't try too hard to rotate – otherwise you may twist too much, making the landing difficult. Throw your head over your shoulder and look through the turn (as I am doing in the main shot).

Step 5 To land, get the nose of the board pointing towards the beach. Hold on tight and get back into trim position.

Quick Tips
1. Use the wave's momentum.
2. Don't try too hard if it's big – the wave's power should do most of the work for you.
3. Focus on where you are trying to hit.
4. Throw your head in the direction of the rotation.
5. Hold on tight and get your weight back on the inside rail to ride out of the move.

INTERMEDIATE

CUT BACK TO FORWARD SPIN

Known as a "cuttie forward", this move is very functional for getting you back to the critical section from the shoulder of a wave.

• As you trim out onto the shoulder, aim for the top third of the wall and initiate your cutback.

• Try to look back in the direction that you have just come from and transfer your weight from your inside rail to your outside rail. The board should now be on its rail edge displacing water and creating a spray fan.

• Now quickly flatten your board so that you come off your rail edge and are riding with the bottom of your board totally flat on the wave's face.

• At this point you will almost feel as though you come to a complete standstill for a millisecond. In a fluid motion slide your weight forward, bring your legs up and cross them to your backside and at the same time throw your head in the direction that you want to spin (in an up-the-wave direction).

• Try to keep your legs crossed all the way through the spin, then when you are facing back down the line drop them from their crossed position, put your weight back on your inside rail by leaning all your weight down your elbow, lean forward and gain speed.

• You should now be racing out of the pocket and ready to look for your next move.

SITTING ON YOUR BOARD

When you are hanging out in the line-up for any length of time, the best way to catch your breath and gain a decent view of the oncoming waves is to sit up on your board.

The first step is to slide your weight forward then, grabbing your board on each side about 30 centimetres from the nose, slowly slide the board down under the water between your legs until there is an equal amount of board in front of you and behind you.

Try to relax and centre your weight so that it's on your buttocks. Keep your back straight. The more you tense, the more you'll wobble. Try to look forwards instead of down. After you feel as though you have your balance, release your grip on your board. With plenty of practice you'll find your balance point and it will become second nature. Sitting on your board is a great way to open up your lungs and catch your breath after a heavy paddle, but don't get caught in the trap of sitting there daydreaming. Stay busy in the line-up to catch plenty of waves!

TIM JONES

REVERSE SPIN

THE REVERSE SPIN, REMEMBER TO TRY TO KEEP YOUR LEGS CROSSED THROUGH OUT THE MOVE.

The reverse is a move that can be carried out more or less anywhere on the wave and can be as easy or as hard as you want it to be. As long as you keep your legs crossed and look in the direction of the manoeuvre, it should look stylish no matter where it's attempted.

Step 1
As with all manoeuvres, a good bottom turn is important. The reverse is no different, although when first getting to grips with the move only a slight bottom turn is required. If you come off the bottom too sharply you risk being directed off the back before having time to complete the rotation – consequently, the shoulder is an ideal place to practice as there's no rush to complete the move before the next section breaks. Bottom turn and then, immediately afterwards, move slightly forwards on your board and initiate the spinning motion by simultaneously lifting your hips and legs from the water and throwing your head in the direction of the turn (i.e. back towards the breaking part of the wave).

Step 2
Once spinning, try to keep your legs crossed – not only will the move look a lot better, but you have less chance of a random limb catching the face and digging in. You can control the speed of the spin by how far from the wave you lift your legs and how long you keep them up for.

Step 3
When you have spun far enough move back to a normal trim position, place your legs back on to the surface, and look in the direction you want to be travelling next. Reverses like the one pictured (although not exactly critical) make the best of a weak section and are an eye-catching alternative to a cutback or turn.

QUICK TIPS
- As you come out of your bottom turn, release your inside rail and centre your weight.
- Cross your legs tightly to show good style.
- Arch your back and throw your head into the direction that you want to spin.
- As you complete the spin, drop your legs to help regain your edge control.
- Re-position your weight back down through your shoulder and into your elbow to re-engage your edge.
- Pull your weight forward on the board and continue to trim back down the line.

MICKEY SMITH

INTERMEDIATE

FORWARD SPINS

ONE OF BODYBOARDINGS MOST FUN MOVES, THE FORWARD SPIN.

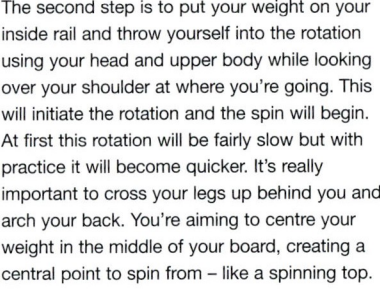

The 360 is a benchmark move that look good if done with the right style in the critical section of the wave. They are an important part of many combination manoeuvres, and one of the most enjoyable basic moves to learn.

Step 1
Like any move speed is essential but, unlike most moves, it has to be controlled – when you're learning to do spins, speed can make the move more difficult.

Spinners can be performed after a cutback to produce an impressive combination move or on a sloping part of the wave. If the move is performed in a flat section it makes it more difficult (and looks lame). When you've gained a bit of speed, the first step is to release the rail. This is done by bottom turning towards the top of the wave, flattening your board out and lifting your legs out of the water.

Step 2
The second step is to put your weight on your inside rail and throw yourself into the rotation using your head and upper body while looking over your shoulder at where you're going. This will initiate the rotation and the spin will begin. At first this rotation will be fairly slow but with practice it will become quicker. It's really important to cross your legs up behind you and arch your back. You're aiming to centre your weight in the middle of your board, creating a central point to spin from – like a spinning top.

Step 3
To complete the manoeuvre you need to return to the direction you were heading. Stop the spin by dropping your flippers back into the water and returning to the standard trim position – you can then bottom turn back into the trim.

If the manoeuvre has been performed on a steep part of the wave then you should shift your weight down onto the bottom corner of your board so you don't nose-dive when you come back down the wave.

Once mastered you can start to perform 360s on different parts of the wave and – not only will you have learnt the prerequisite to entering competitions – but you will look pretty smooth to your mate paddling back out!

TAKE OFF ROLL

The take off roll is an old school gem that is often forgotten but always worth having in the bag. One of bodyboarding's first stunts, you could bring it back with friends for kicks or for a rad perspective in meaty shoreys! You want to be under the wave as it is already pitching: the lip should be just throwing over your head while you're static down in the pit looking up. Now look over your outside shoulder, board and body immersed in the wave face and, using the suck of water up the face of the tube, let your head lead in the direction the lip's pitching and let the slab throw you up and over. Enjoy the split second view and subsequent hilarious beating. Endless hours of neck-breaking fun!.

1 JACK JOHNS TAKE OFF EL ROLLO.

ROCK ENTRY

TIME YOUR LEAP SO THAT YOU LAND OVER THE BACK OF THE INCOMING WAVE WHERE THE WATER IS AT ITS DEEPEST.

Entry to some breaks (particularly reef breaks) may require a sketchy clamber across slimy dangerous rocks. It's really easy to fall over, so the key is to concentrate on where every foot is going to be placed and to use your board as a walking aid.

Place your board into handy rock crevices so that as you take each step you can put your weight on the board, helping you to get a safe footing before transferring your weight. It sounds simple, but bear in mind you are usually negotiating swell washing over the rocks, urchins in the crevices and rocks covered in slime…using your board as a walking aid can be an absolute lifesaver!

ANOTHER ALTERNATE USE FOR YOUR BODYBOARD - A WALKING AID!

Entering the water from the rocks
When you've successfully negotiated the walk across the rocks the next stage – entering the water – can be equally tricky.

1. The key is to locate a ledge of rock with a drop-off into the deepest possible area of water. Watch the spot for a couple of sets and when the water recedes (just after a wave has washed in and it washes out again) check the area for dangerous looking exposed rocks.

2+3. When you find a safe entry point, wait for a wave to come towards you – the last wave of a set is best. Time your leap so that you land on the back of the wave as it's coming towards you. It is essential to keep the board pointing out towards the horizon so that it creates the least resistance to the oncoming wave as possible. If you hesitate, then wait for the next wave and try again. Do not jump into the water as the wave begins to drain back out to sea again, as the water will be at its most shallow at this point and you'll literally hit rock bottom.

4+5. Your leap needs to be well-timed, committed and your board needs to be under your body. That way, if the worst happens, at least you will land on your board on top of a rock instead of impaling yourself.

6. As you hit the water, start paddling for the horizon. It's important not to take deep strokes though. Just take shallow kicks with your feet or stroke out with your arm. Enter the water knowing where you're heading - there's no time to dither when you're close to a rock shelf with waves breaking on it. That's why it's best to wait for the last wave of a set - then there should be an easy paddle. Remember, never enter the water without knowing where you plan to exit it from. It can be a lot harder to get out than to get in!

ROCK EXIT

REMEMBER TO CHECK BEHIND YOU SO THAT YOU DON'T GET KNOCKED OVER BY A SNEAKY WAVE.

Exiting the water over a rock bottom
At lots of reefbreaks and some beachbreaks you will have to leave the water by riding up a rock shelf. Follow these steps for a safe exit.

1. Before you enter the water determine your exit point and stick to your plan unless the conditions change. It's best to have a back-up plan just in case your original exit becomes too dangerous.

2. Catch a wave in (don't try to paddle in between sets as you may get caught out). Try to choose one of the last waves of a set.
3. As you near the rocks, stall your board by lifting the nose and sinking the tail. This will slow you down and let the foam surround you. Make sure that by the time you get to the rock platform you aren't out the front of the whitewater, but you have stalled enough for you to be in the middle to top third of the foam.

4. Allow yourself to run aground on to the rock and then – using your board as a platform – push up from the ground and stand up. Don't worry about your board – it's a resilient piece of kit – just be conscious that you need to be moving fairly quickly and get on your feet fast. Get up drop-knee style so that your fin doesn't get caught and trip you up. Move quickly and decisively.

5. As soon as you are on your feet, check behind you for the next wave: if you know where it is you can either hurry forwards out of its way or brace yourself for the impact!

6. When the coast is clear, walk to safety, hopefully with your dignity still intact!

BODYBOARD MANUAL

INTERMEDIATE

CUT BACKS

CUTTING BACK TO THE POWER POCKET.

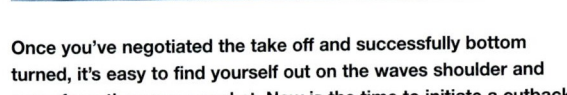

Once you've negotiated the take off and successfully bottom turned, it's easy to find yourself out on the waves shoulder and away from the power pocket. Now is the time to initiate a cutback.

Step 1
To get a nice fan of water you need to have a reasonable amount of speed so it's best to set yourself up with a nice bottom turn. Then gun it down the line positioning yourself about midway up the face of the wave.

Step 2
Shift your weight to your outside rail, quite far back near the tail of the board. Lead your board through the turn with your front hand. Arch your back and keep focused on the direction that you're heading.

Step 3
Now that you've shifted all you weight onto the rail you should produce a glorious fan of water! The more speed you have and the harder you jam your rail in, the bigger the fan should be. You'll use all your speed at this part of your turn, giving the wave a chance to catch up with you.

Step 4
Now that you're spent, position yourself back on your inside rail as you would normally ride and continue on down the wave...

QUICK TIPS – CUTBACKS
- Ride into the move with maximum speed.
- Shift your weight smoothly from rail to rail for a slick turn.
- Watch where you're going, don't stare at your spray!
- When you're back in the power pocket, adjust your weight back into the speed trim position and eye the next section down the line.

TRIMMING

The most exhilarating part of bodyboarding is gaining speed. To do this you must position yourself in a functional trim position. The following steps will help you gain a functional trim.

IN TRIM.

Step 1
Choose the direction that you wish to travel on the wave. Look down the line and focus on the direction that you're going to travel.

Step 2
Your leading hand should grip the front inside corner of your board (the side closest to the wave face). You should slide your weight forward and your other hand should grip – or lay flat on the deck next to – the outside rail of your board. Your leading forearm should be laid flat on the deck of your board on its side. Your wrist should be twisted and 'cocked' so that the fingers gripping the corner of the board can pull slightly on the nose (which enables more pressure to be applied) with your elbow creating projection from your board. Your weight should be distributed down your shoulder and into your elbow. This will push the rail into the wave, displacing water and gaining what is referred to as an 'edge' in the wave.

Step 3
Your outside arm doesn't need to pull up on the opposite rail edge unless you are bottom turning. Just hold the rail with your elbow poked out at a right angle. It's important to move far enough forward for your hips to be positioned on the deck of the board, just up from the tail. Keep your legs straight out behind you. Only let them drag if you want to slow down or gain increased control – i.e. if the wave suddenly gets much steeper.

Step 4
Keep your back arched, head up and shoulders square - with your inside shoulder slightly further forward than the other. Lunging with your head and shoulders (known as the 'Chicken Head') will help you to gain speed.

BOTTOM TURNS

THE FOUNDATIONS OF ALL GOOD BODYBOARDING MOVES BEGIN WITH A SOLID BOTTOM TURN.

A good bottom turn is the key to good bodyboarding. The top guys can really be noticed by the ease and smoothness that they convert the speed that they've gained from dropping into a wave into down-the-line speed.

Step 1
The common misconception with bottom turning is that, like surfers, you fly down the wave straight and then crank a sharp bottom turn to head back up to the lip. This makes it very difficult to hold your speed, and bodyboarders need to approach the turn differently. Angled takeoffs with a smooth direction change are much more effective.

Step 2
When you feel that you've caught the wave, move forward into the trim position and ride down the wave at an angle. The bottom turn is the act of engaging the rail in the wave face and converting speed from one direction to the other, so the emphasis is on keeping the turn smooth and skip-free. When you are ready to initiate the turn (as you reach the bottom half of the wave), begin to lean your shoulder over towards the wave face, arch your back and focus on drawing an unbroken line with your rail.

Step 3
A good bottom turn sees none of the rider's body touching the water through the turn (except maybe their legs). If your elbow or shoulder touches the water it will slow you down by creating drag. Many riders bend their outside leg at the knee through the bottom turn. It is now that you can use your outside hand to pull up slightly on the rail. The steeper the wave, the more that the rail will need to be pulled up.

Step 4
Most British waves will need a reasonably slight angled bottom turn. Wedgy or reef waves require a more forced, defined turn. In bigger waves the bottom turn can be one of the harder moves in bodyboarding and definitely the most important as it's an integral part of all moves.

BASICS

GETTING THROUGH WAVES AND DUCK DIVING

Getting out through the waves is a fundamental yet deceptively difficult aspect of becoming a good bodyboarder.

GUIDE YOUR BOARD THROUGH THE DUCK DIVE TO AVOID THE TURBULENCE OF THE WAVE OVER HEAD.

To get through waves as your paddling out back, you'll have to make a decision as to whether you go under or over them.

To go over the top of a broken wave (whitewater). Paddle towards the wave at speed and, when it gets within half a metre of you, lift the nose of your board up about 20cm (a little more for big 'uns). Then let the wave do the work as it flows underneath you. Keep on paddling throughout and avoid the mistake that many beginners make – lifting the nose of their board about half a metre out of the water - this creates resistance to the oncoming wave and allows it to smash you backward towards the shore or, worse still, hit you in the face.

Step 2 If an oncoming line of whitewater is particularly big or a wave is about to break on top of you, then a duckdive is required. Again, paddle towards the wave at speed. When you get about two metres away slide your weight forward and move your hands about 30cm down from the nose, holding tightly onto the rails. Push up into a press-up position with your head directly over the nose of your board. As your board begins to sink, shove your knee into the tail to guide it downwards. Stretch your other leg out behind you. If your timing is good, the wave should now break over you. Now lay flat against your board and look up at the whitewater as it passes over you (see shot 2).

Step 3 When it's passed, move your weight further back on your board and angle upwards (see shot 4). The whole time that you are underwater you should kick with your fins to avoid being dragged back. The bigger the wave is, the earlier you should aim to become submerged. The main hazard with duckdiving at shallow reefs is hitting the reef by going too deep. Avoid this by keeping your hands flat on the board's deck or by clutching the board's rails – don't put them underneath (see shot 1).

The key to getting out back quickly is timing and wave knowledge. Try to avoid the bigger set waves by timing their frequency and use channels to your advantage (but beware of rip currents). You'll get it in the end!

PADDLING

The secret of easy paddling is to develop a rhythm, either using your arms and legs alternately, or both arms and legs together. When you're paddling through flat water it's a good opportunity to use your arms, and when you're paddling through turbulent water use your legs. When you need to get somewhere quickly use both your arms and legs.

Leg Paddling
Your hips should be off the back of the board with the whole of your leg submerged under the water. Your hands should be holding the front corners of the board. Your board should be flat on the water so that you glide along instead of pushing water. This may mean applying a bit of pressure with your hands. Your back should be arched and your chest upright. Kick with the whole of your legs, keeping them completely immersed all the time. It's the downward stroke that gives you the thrust. Concentrate on long drawn out 'quality' strokes rather than quick, short kicks.

Arm Paddling
Move your body forward on your board and keep your legs straight and together behind you. Your face should almost be in line with the nose of your board. Arch your back and keep your head up, watching where you're going. Use the front crawl style stroke – alternate arms – reaching as far forward as you can and diving your arm as deep as possible, drawing each stroke as far back as you can each time. Keep your fingers slightly apart as the vortex created draws more water into your hand. It's the last half of each stroke that has the most forward thrust so really dig in towards the end of each rhythm. Aim to keep your body still and let your arms do the work.

Combined Leg and Arm Paddling
For maximum propulsion (taking maximum effort!), position yourself just back from where you lie to arm paddle. Lower your head and chest to keep the nose of the board flat on the water and then paddle with your legs and arms. It's tricky to balance at first but gets much easier with practice. This is the preferred technique of many pros to catch waves.

ARM PADDLING, GREAT FOR FLAT WATER PADDLING.

ARMS STRAIGHT AND LEGS PREDOMINANTLY UNDER THE SURFACE, THE KEY TO GOOD PADDLING.

Balancing Act

Lots of beginner bodyboarders have trouble balancing on their boards. This is usually because they're too far forward. This problem can be overcome by positioning your body with your hips off the back of the tail. Hold on to the front two corners of your board with either hand. Your index and second fingers should be positioned over the nose the other two fingers over the board's rail. Your thumbs should spread towards the centre of your board and your arms should be straight – resting on the deck of the board.

The common mistake is to be too far up the board with your arms bent. The straighter that your arms are, the better the balance is that you'll have and the better you'll paddle. The more of your legs that are in the water the better so you'll be able to kick. Also, if your elbows are hanging off the side of your board then you're too far forward and will have poor balance and probably drag, which will slow you down further.

Strapping On

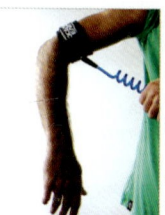

Putting your leash on can be tricky. Many people don't realise that you need to put it on with the cord coming away from the inside of your arm - i.e. on the thumb side. This will enable the leash to sit on the deck of the board rather than in the water creating drag. Always try to buy a coiled leash, they stay out of the way much more effectively. Put the leash on top of your wetsuit (don't roll it up and put it underneath). If the leash is a bicep coil, place it just above your elbow or just above your bicep muscle. Again the cord should be coming away from the inside of your arm. If it's a wrist leash place it just past your wrist joint. Remove your watch if it's on that arm.

As far as fin tethers are concerned, attach them just above your ankle. Roll up your wettie leg first and put them under there. Roll your wetsuit back down over the top – this will help them stay done up, and greatly reduce the amount of drag that they cause. Many riders prefer shoe laces tying their fins to their ankle instead of velcro fin savers.

Rub Avoidance

If you're surfing a lot then even the best fitting wetsuit can begin to rub. Deal with it straight away or it'll turn in to a nightmare... If it's on your upper body, get yourself a rash vest and apply Vaseline to the troublesome area.

One of the biggest problem areas is the back of the knee. Rubs here can get so bad that they'll stop you being able to walk properly if you don't deal with them early enough. They won't go away on their own so get yourself some Lycra trousers – try sports shops that sell aerobics kit. If you can't find any then pull your wetsuit up to just above your knee then get a dollop of Vaseline on your hand and slide it down to the trouble zone. If you put it on before pulling up your suit it'll just get rubbed off. If you're surfing without a suit on be prepared to get a bit of belly rash for the first few sessions – after that it'll usually go away. If you get rub on your bare forearms, rub a thick layer of wax into that area of the deck of your board.

HOW TO PLUG YOUR BOARD

• **Decide where the plug is to go.** This is determined by which arm you are going to wear your leash on, where your front foot is to go if you are going to ride in the drop knee stance and where your leash plug was positioned on your last board (if it worked there then put it in the same place again, if it didn't then adjust it!).

Has the board got stringers? If it has then locate where they are (there should be information about this from the manufacturer on the board's packaging) or ask the shop that you bought the board from. Stringers must be avoided when leash plugging! Sometimes if you hold a board up to a bright light you can see the stringer as a dark shadow running through the board.

• **In shot one 1 I have positioned my old board on top of my new board.** I have removed my old leash plug so that I can poke a Phillips (crosshead) screwdriver through the old hole and make a mark on my new board. As long as your new board is pretty much the same shape as your old one then this will work. If you have gone for a drastic change in template – a DK board for instance – then this won't work.

• **Avoiding the stringers in the board, your leash hole should be about 20cm back from the nose of the board, towards the centre.** If you look at the bottom of the board, make sure that the plug isn't going to be positioned so that it is on the curve of the slick-skin's rocker. Do not plug your board near the rail as it will get in the way of your arm when you are trimming and also be weaker and more likely to pull through.

• **Lay your board flat on the floor and drive the screwdriver straight down until you feel it pushing against the skin on the bottom of the board.** It is essential to make sure the screwdriver goes in straight or the leash plug won't connect when you insert it.

• **Now stand the board up and push the screwdriver through from the other side.** You will see where to pierce the skin as there will be a mark.

• **Wiggle the screwdriver around a little so that the hole is big enough for the plug to go into.**

• **Now place the top of the plug in the hole on the deck side of the board and attach the screw through the other side.** Use a 2p or 10p coin to tighten it up.

BASICS

QUICK TIPS

Here are some first-steps to help smooth your path into a fun bodyboarding lifestyle and avoid any embarrassing hiccups!

Cover up
Get yourself a board sock. They protect your board from dings and heat and you can use it as a towel when you get out of the water.

How Not To Face Plant
Walking in swim fins when you're not used to them can be pretty challenging at first. The trick is to take really exaggerated steps. Bring your knees up higher than you usually would, and walk in a kind of skipping action so they don't get caught as you bring your foot through. After a while you'll do it without even thinking, but until then you need to concentrate or you'll end up face first in the sand – not a good look.

When you get to ankle depth water turn around and start walking backwards. Don't lift your feet off the floor though. Just slide them along the bottom in a kind of moon-walk movement. Keep looking over your shoulder in the direction that you're going and try to step into the waves as they hit you.

Hold your board with your hands on the front corners of the nose and the tail resting in the water. This will offer least resistance to the incoming waves so as they hit you there's less chance of you getting knocked over. As soon as you get to waist-depth water you can start paddling.

Remember to de-slime
When you buy sunscreen look for the non-greasy stuff. Whenever you apply cream, make sure you wipe your hands on a towel (or a board sock) before hitting the water - otherwise your hands will slip off your rails.

Fin Rubs
If you feel a fin rub coming on then deal with it straight away – if left untreated it could ruin your summer. Clean it using antiseptic, let it get plenty of air, and then stop it from being rubbed any further. Buy some rubberised patches from the chemist to put on before you hit the water.

Shake the Socks
If you've never bodyboarded without your socks on, then give it a try – they cause a lot more drag than you would expect and your legs will feel lighter without them. If flipper rubs are a concern then cover your heel strap with neoprene (which you can get from wetsuit manufacturers) and sew it on. Then take your fins to the shoe repair shop, and get them to glue the neoprene inside the foot pocket on for you.

Stay Springy
If you've got a coiled leash, recoil it after use and fasten it with the Velcro to keep its spring.

Food For Thought
If you're having a summer surf marathon and you can only bring yourself to get out of the water for a quick snack, go for a banana and plenty of water. The banana will quickly convert to energy, and the water will keep you hydrated and help to fend off cramp.

Traction Action
When you get a new wetsuit you may find it really slippery against your board. If you don't mind your suit getting a worn-in look straight away, get a bar of wax and rub it on your hips and stomach area. The suit should then be nice and grippy.

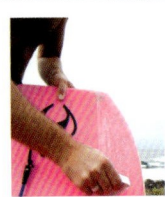

Dry Wettie?
The best way to dry out your wetsuit is to hang it on a plastic hanger (metal ones get rusty and spoil your suit) and leave it in the sun. When you store your winter suit, leave it hanging somewhere, if you fold it and leave it stuffed in a cupboard then the creases can ruin the rubber.

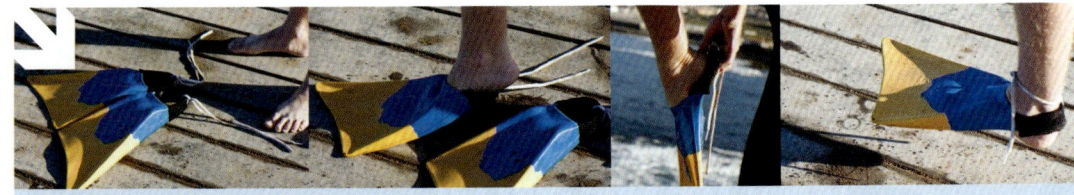

PUTTING YOUR FINS ON
• make sure that the fins are the correct way up and the right and left foot are in the right place (there are usually little written instructions on the fins to show this).
• standing in front of the fins, slide one of your feet all the way inside as far as it will go.
• standing on one foot pull the heel strap around the back of your ankle.
• repeat the process with your second fin.
• attach your fin-saver or tie up your fin-string.

When choosing a board your main considerations should be?
1 Where are you using it?
2 What size do you need? Your height v weight ratio. Length should be between your hip and naval with increased width in the board for heavier riders
3 Price? The right board will be easier to ride and will be better constructed – so it's worth saving up and getting a top-end board. Your riding will progress quicker and your board will last longer. You can probably purchase one for £100 that will have all of the performance you need and will be as good as many of the more expensive boards on the market. Paying for top end isn't always necessary. – DH

Remember…
• The price of the boards is relative to the performance and quality of materials.
• Make sure you are completely honest about your ability when talking to a sales assistant.
• Make sure you get the right size board, a rough size guide can be found on the bottom of most boards but the sales assistant should know the correct size straight away.
• Use a specialist bodyboard shop that has a good choice of boards: your perfect board will be there somewhere.
• Size is relative to your weight and height. Refer to the size guide but also ask the sales assistant or go with an experienced friend.

RAILS
There are two main types of rails: 60/40 this means the bottom part of the rail is 60% and the top is 40% – the bigger the bottom rail, the more control you get. 50/50 is an evenly distributed rail that is slightly looser.

Both combinations work well and it's just down to personal preference, but many brands tend to favour the 60/40 rail. – **AB**

Always look for double rails, two layers of foam bonded together. This construction will stiffen the rail and will help prevent the board from creasing and it also helps to make the board faster. – **DH**

WIDE BOARDS V NARROW
A good all round board will tend to have a slightly more rounded appearance when you look at it face on. This more rounded shape makes the board easier to turn, especially for slower speed moves. Also, the extra width helps to sit the board a little higher in the water which means less drag therefore better in small to medium size surf.

Narrow boards do have the advantage of more speed and control in faster surf, and are great for moves performed on more critical sections of the wave. It is important to be realistic about the type of waves you are surfing before choosing a narrow template though… – **DH**

What difference does the position of the board's wide point makes?
The wide point on the board changes the whole template shape. A high wide point keeps the width on the nose - combining this with a wide tail make the rails really straight giving you down the line speed. Moving the wide point down the board and having a smaller tail width gives a rounder template that loosens the board, both great for prone riding and drop knee where you would have the wide point nearer the middle where your knee goes… – **AB**

TO SUMMARISE
You need to think about the following 3 things, the 3 F's:

• Flatness
• Flex
• Floatation

Is the board flat? Does it have the correct flex for the conditions you are using it in? Does the board have enough floatation for your size and the conditions you're surfing it in?

Make sure the board is the correct length for you. If it is too long you will have to move your body much more to gain speed and your hips won't be able to control the tail, which will cause you to side slip. It will also be harder to catch waves.

A board that is too short will simply not have enough floatation and again will be harder to catch waves on.

Finally, only buy from a reputable shop with experience of riding and selling bodyboards. These are expensive bits of foam and buying the right board will help you progress much quicker and ensure that you have much more fun when you're riding! – **DH**

makes the board looser which is good for spinning. Remember that looser can also be a disadvantage though, as you don't have as much control especially in steeper waves – **BM**

SLICK/BOTTOM SKIN?

Hands down still the best bottom material for any climate is surlyn, manufactured by DuPont. Surlyn has elastic properties which ensure that the board springs back to its original shape after it's flexed. This material is also quite forgiving and does not crease as much as boards that use HTPE bottom skins. Surlyn is the original and still the best, always look for this material if you are buying a board for over £90. **– DH**

People tend to overlook slicks on their boards but it's got to be surlyn slicks every time! It costs a little bit more but it's well worth the extra. It is extremely durable making it less prone to creasing and - due to its rubbery properties – offers perfect flex and recoil for increased projection. Sweet. **– AB**

ROCKER?

The thing to note about rocker is the following:

Too much rocker will make the board push water and it will become much harder to ride, the ideal board is nice and flat with a bit of lift in the top 8-10 inches.

Make sure you get a board with correct flex for the climate you're using it in. When you need curve (rocker) you should be able to bend it into the board whilst riding.

The thing to avoid is negative rocker – which means a board that is inverted or convex. If you start with negative rocker the chances are it will only get worse and you will end up with a slow board that'll be harder to ride.

Take a look at the edge of the board – along the rails – to check how flat it is. Don't be sold a dud! **– DH**

I think riders should be looking for a flat board with just enough rocker in the nose to stop you nose diving. The board be able to flex according to the wave shape. **– BM**

JACK JOHNS TEST DRIVING HIS CUSTOM SHAPE IN IRELAND.

BASICS

BOARDS

BY DAVE HEARD

WE DECIDED TO PUT FOUR BRITISH BODYBOARD SALESMEN ON THE SPOT AND FIND OUT A BIT ABOUT WHAT THEY FELT ARE THE BEST DESIGN FEATURES AND MATERIALS FOR OUR CHILLY BRITISH WATERS.

Our bodyboard geeks are:
Adam Bailey (AB), Overhead Surf
Brooke Mason (BM), Down The Line
Joel Whitmore (JW), Bournemouth Surfing Centre
Dave Heard (DH), Bodyboard HQ

THE WORLDS MOST FAMOUS BODYBOARD SHAPER; NICK 'MEZ' MESRITZ IN ACTION.

As well as a description of the different bodyboard features and materials to keep your eyes out for, we've also included some insider knowledge from the men on the front line who kit people out for a living. So: take heed of these wise words before you step into a shop or start browsing online...

WHICH CORE AND WHY?

The most important part of the construction of your board is the core. The core's ability to flex and spring back to its original shape is the magic that gives the board all of its control and extra speed.

The best core for colder water is constructed of 2.2 pcf pe foam, often referred to as dow. It gives a nice springy flex which works great in colder water. Perfect for 9° to 19° temperature waters. Always consider a board which has a carbon fibre stringer (rod) for extra strength and recall. Some riders prefer the extra weight of pe foam cores as they give the board a more solid feeling on the face of the wave.

For warmer climates or hotter days, consider a 1.9 pcf pp (polypro) core. It is light, strong and water-proof and will last longer. For most riders, it is unsuitable for use in colder waters unless they have a very heavy riding style. It is worth having a pp board for travel: especially for tropical destinations. PP boards are faster but at the expense of manoeuvrability in colder water. – **DH**

DECKS?

For both cold and warm water 8lb (density per square inch)PE works the best. It's softer and of a more open celled construction so doesn't impede the core's ability to bend and spring back. Hence it helps the board to keep its magic flex, recall and projection. There are boards available with closed cell higher density decks, they tend to be very strong but they lack the real magic that makes the board work well. – **DH**

I think 8 pound polyethylene is the best all round deck material on the market. It is strong, responsive, has good recoil properties and when you get your elbow indentations they are spread evenly and not in one straight crease like with the cheaper crosslink materials. – **BM**

CRESCENT TAIL?

The crescent tail still functions as the best all round tail design available. It is great for all types of surf and for beginners to expert alike. It is also great for drop knee riding. The things to note with crescent tail designs are the following: the deeper the crescent, the more hold and grip you get but the less floatation – therefore less speed especially in smaller surf.

The smaller the tail peg, the more grip you get. The wider the tail peg, the bigger turning area you get so the board becomes more manoeuvrable for spins and other sliding moves. – **DH**

The crescent tail gives a lot of bite into the wave face and more rail to rail control. Great for DK and charging bigger, steeper slabs. – **JW**

SQUARE TAIL?

The square tail is a bit of a no man's land and tends to lack grip and control. This tail design is often applied to very cheap boards, due to its simplicity of manufacture. It is rarely used on better boards. – **DH**

BAT TAIL?

The bat tail is great for prone riding. It is especially good in smaller surf and is also a good choice for heavier riders. The bat tail will give you increased surface area and floatation which means more speed and less drag. It is also a looser tail design so great for slower speed moves. The down side of this is less control especially in faster surf. Some bat tails have exaggerated hooked tail pegs, these give a better blend of both speed and control – **DH**

The advantages of a bat tail is that it makes the board faster and it also

EQUIPMENT

A bodyboard, leash, fins and a wetsuit are your essentials for riding a few waves... Although there are plenty of other accessories that you can buy! We'd recommend the following kit for a comfortable bodyboarding life in the UK's intemperate climate:

Leashes
The main choices are between a wrist or bicep Velcro attachment. When making a purchase check the Velcro attachments and if it's a top end model look for brass 'swivels' on the joints of the leash that stop it getting tangled too often. Make sure you get a quality "smooth top" leash plug with your purchase as well.

Fins
If you're going to take bodyboarding seriously then a decent pair of well-fitting fins will be essential. Prices range from £20 to £55 and the more you pay the better the fins will be. Always rinse them out in fresh water to ensure that they last and try to pick a fin that is stiff in the blade and soft, comfortable and well-fitting in the foot pocket. If you wear neoprene fin socks then take them along to the shop with you and wear 'em when you try on the fin. In the summer it's great to shed as much neoprene as possible, so try to go for a pair of fins that will fit comfortably without your socks as well. Ideally you'll have bigger fins that fit with socks for winter, and smaller fins that fit without socks for the summer.

Flipper Slippers
A great option for summer use. Enjoy lighter feet due to a reduced amount of neoprene but still benefit from rub protection.

Rash Vest
Go for a compressed neoprene rash vest with titanium lining and Lycra rash protection – you'll benefit from increased warmth and be rub free.

Fin Socks
Fin socks keep your feet warm in the winter and offer protection from nasty fin rubs. The fin socks with the screen print on the bottom are recommended as the soles don't wear through as quickly.

Wax
A liberal layer of wax on a new board should keep the board grippy for a good few weeks use. Apply wax heavily where you're going to hold the board and liberally where movement is essential (on the deck where your stomach is going to be).

BUYING A WETSUIT
A wetsuit is a vital piece of kit for bodyboarding in Britain. Here are some tips for getting the best suit for your needs at the right price.

Step 1 Decide where you're going to use the suit and for which season. In the south of England you can get away with a 3/2mm thick wetsuit during the summer months and a 5/3mm suit in the winter. In the north you'll need a 5/3mm (or thicker) all year round. Seek advice from the shop assistant or better still, ask an impartial local surfer what they use. Decide your price range by calculating the amount of use that you expect to get out of it. The more that you are willing to pay, the warmer, longer lasting and more flexible the suit will be.

Step 2 Probably the most important feature of a wetsuit is that it fits you. The seals on the wrists, ankles and neck need to be tight but comfortable. It's important that the suit has no baggy areas or big wrinkles otherwise water will sit in these 'cold zones' and make you chilly. If a sales assistant tries to tell you that it's okay to have a suit that you'll grow into, don't believe them. Suits that don't fit are cold and uncomfortable. Always go for a suit that fits and try to negotiate a trade in deal if you're likely to grow out of it in six months.

Step 3 Once you've chosen the most comfortable suit in your price range, ask about the warranty against materials and manufacture - if the card needs stamping by the retailer get it done, pay up and get out there!

BASICS

HEAD INJURIES

Head Injuries are the last thing on your mind when it's pumping and you're having a great session. But if your friend came off a wave and hit the bottom, or their board caught them on the head - would you know how to establish whether they had a serious head injury, and would you know what to do if they had? Stuart Parry (RLSS Assessor, NARS trainer) gives us the lowdown on what to look for and what to do.

HISTORY, SIGNS, SYMPTOMS

History - How did they do it? If they can't tell you, then try to establish how they injured themselves – ask other people, or check their board to see if it's damaged.

Signs – Check for obvious signs of trauma (lumps, bumps, bleeding), and check to see if the pupils are the same size. If not, then this could be a sign of concussion.

Symptoms – These could include slurred speech, dizziness, laboured breathing or nausea.

Treatment

If you can see any of the signs and symptoms listed above then the patient needs to be checked over by a medical professional immediately. Get the lifeguard, call 999, or get a member of the public to call if you don't have your phone. Make sure that you tell anyone who attends that you think they make have a head injury, and explain why you think this.

Try and keep them immobilised where you find them and keep monitoring their level of consciousness by talking to them and reassuring them. If the casualty starts to lose consciousness then get them to lie on the ground (if they are not already) so they don't do further damage. Keep checking the patient, make sure they are warm enough (if not, then cover them with a coat or blanket) and reassure them.

Ask the casualty whether they have any neck or lower back pain, or if they have any tingling in their fingers. If the answer to any of these questions is yes, then you need to immobilise the head and the neck and treat the patient as a spinal injury. To immobilise the head, place your hands on either side of their head but don't cover the ears (so that they can still hear you!). Your aim is to keep the head and neck in alignment.

In the worst case scenario – if the patient becomes unconscious and stops breathing – you must commence CPR at a rate of 30 compressions to 2 breaths.

So, the key things are to quickly establish whether the patient has any of the symptoms of a head injury, and if so seek medical attention immediately and keep the patient still. And remember that alcohol and drugs can mask a serious head injury.

ThreeSixty have teamed up with Era Adventures to help you to do the responsible thing and follow a lifeguard or first aid course - you never know when you'll need the skills to save a mate's life (see the ad on page 21). Quote 'ThreeSixty magazine' when booking your lifeguard, surf instructor or first aid course, and receive a voucher to take a mountain biking course, a coasteering session, a surf coaching session, or a bodyboarding lesson absolutely free.

Go to www.threesixtymag.co.uk for further details or phone 01637 878074.

LIFEGUARDS PATROLLING AT FISTRAL BEACH.

FIRST AID AND RE-SUS

d. Keep checking the pulse. Stop chest compression as soon as a pulse returns.
NEVER start chest compression if the heart is beating.
DO NOT GIVE UP until medical assistance arrives.

BLEEDING
If the victim has a bad cut, raise the part of the body which is bleeding (if possible), and use a clean pad to apply direct external pressure to the site of the wound. Seek medical help immediately.

HYPOTHERMIA
Immersion in cold water can lead to hypothermia if the body temperature drops below 95°F. Both the nervous system and muscles are affected so symptoms may include shivering, slurred speech, and difficulty in thinking clearly. If the condition becomes severe, death can result through heart failure so immediate action is necessary. Get assistance from the lifeguards and call an ambulance. Remove the victim's wet clothing or wetsuit, and warm up his body by covering him with dry blankets or clothes. Other ways to raise the body temperature are to place the victim in a lukewarm, body-temperature (not hot) bath, or to share your own body heat by getting into a sleeping bag together.

HEAD INJURIES
A casualty does not have to have bumps, bleeding or deformity around the head to have a serious head injury. Once again, if in doubt seek medical attention immediately.

Three important terms relating to head injuries are:
Concussion: Violent Shaking of the brain.
Lucid Interval: Time it takes for swelling to Occur.
Compression: Swelling of the brain.
If you come across somebody with a suspected head injury the warning signs to look for are: unequal pupils, change in colour, nausea, dizziness, vomiting, drowsiness, double vision, fitting, slurred speech, repetition or memory loss.
If you notice any change in a casualty's behaviour following a blow to the head, then get help immediately.

SPINAL INJURIES
The symptom of a spinal injury may include: neck & lower back pain, numbness in fingers.

Damage to the spinal cord can result in paralysis or even death. If you suspect the casualty has a spinal injury then minimise movement immediately. Find out as much as you can about how the injury occurred so that you can tell the emergency services when they arrive.

BASICS

EMERGENCIES

How many times have you watched "999 Lifesavers" and heard some poor bloke who's survived a terrible ordeal using the classic line: "I just never thought it would happen to me!" Accidents do happen, it's a fact of life, and whether they're caused by foolishness or plain bad luck makes no difference. At the end of the day the guys who handle tough situations are the guys who know what to do in an emergency.

The following is only intended as a basic guide to emergency action and you should try to get the attention of a lifeguard or call the coastguard as soon as possible. You should also do a course in water safety, rescue skills and resuscitation. The question you should ask yourself is this: if your best mate was in serious trouble, would you know what to do to help?

Check www.era-adventures.co.uk for further info about courses.

WATER RESCUE PROCEDURE

If you're on the beach or in the water and you see or hear someone in distress, you may need to perform a water rescue. Here's what to do:

1. Assess the situation. Do NOT risk your own life if you are not sufficiently experienced in the prevailing conditions. Be especially wary of rip currents, rocks and caves. Establish what needs to be done, and what assistance is needed.

2. Send for help. Alert the lifeguards at the nearest lifeguard station, or phone the coastguard (dial 999). Get assistance from other surfers, especially locals who are likely to be more knowledgeable about the area.

3. If you are completely confident that you can assist the person in trouble without putting your own life at risk, then act quickly. Always use a rescue aid, such as your surfboard or a Peterson tube.

4. The person in trouble may well be distressed or in shock. Talk to them as you approach - try to sound confident, even if you are nervous. When you're about six feet away, pass your board (or rescue aid) to the person. Do not allow them to grab you.

5. Keep the person calm and reassured. If you know help is on its way, it may be best to wait for assistance.

6. If no help is coming, or the situation requires immediate action, place the person on your board and paddle into shore, lying on top of them. Be aware of approaching waves, and keep the patient secure on the board. An unconscious casualty must be brought back to shore as quickly as possible; if they are not breathing, start mouth-to-nose respiration (see below).

8. Once back on the beach, start giving the appropriate aftercare.

THE ABC OF RESUSCITATION

A – Airway Open the airway by lying the person flat on their back, lifting their jaw and after checking that their neck isn't injured, tilting the head back. Carefully remove any obstructions from the mouth.

B – Breathing Check the person is breathing. Look to see if their chest is rising and falling; listen and feel for his breath against your cheek.

C – Circulation Check the pulse. Find the pulse by placing your fingers against the side of the Adam's apple (voice box) and pressing gently down.

• If there is a pulse and the casualty is breathing, put him in the recovery position (lying on his side with the head tilted back to keep the airway open).

• If there is a pulse but no breathing, start mouth-to-mouth (or mouth-to-nose if at sea) respiration:

a. Pinch the casualty's nostrils firmly shut and open the airway.

b. Take a deep breath and seal your lips around the casualty's lips. Blow into the mouth watching the chest rise. Let the chest fall completely. Continue at about 10 breaths per minute, checking the pulse after every 10 breaths.

c. Once the casualty starts breathing, put him in the recovery position.

• If there is no pulse and no breathing, start mouth-to-mouth respiration and chest compression:

a. Give two breaths of mouth-to-mouth.

b. Place the heel of your hand two fingers' breadth above the junction of the rib margin and the sternum (breastbone). Place your other hand on top and interlock your hands.

c. Keeping your arms straight, press down by no more than two inches. Then relax the pressure to allow the heart to refill. Continue at a rate of 80 compressions per minute, but pause every 15 compressions to give two breaths of mouth-to-mouth.

Rob Barber's Bodyboarding School

FOR ALL YOUR BODYBOARDING NEEDS:

DAILY LESSONS
COACHING WEEKENDS
GIRL ONLY COACHING
SUMMER COACHING CAMPS
EQUIPMENT ADVICE
WINTER COACHING TRIPS ABROAD
LESSON VOUCHERS

CHECK ROBBARBER.COM
JOIN OUR FACEBOOK FAN PAGE
CALL: 01637 879571

BASICS

HAZARDS

SURFBOARDS
For beginners, the biggest hazards to watch out for are bodyboards and surfboards that are out of control. If you see someone else's board hurtling towards you, the best course of action is to duck under the water. Surfboards are very buoyant so if you duck two or three feet underwater you'll be safe. Cover your head with your arms as you come up to the surface.

ROCKS
If you're surfing a rocky reef or pointbreak, consider wearing a helmet if it's a really gnarly spot. Try to land feet-first when you wipeout, and never dive off forwards at a shallow break.

WEAVER FISH
Despite their size (six to eight inches long), weaver fish can inflict an excruciatingly painful sting. Weavers are most likely to be encountered at sandy beaches during periods of hot weather, when the fish come into shallow water to spawn. If you get stung (it feels as though you've trodden on a sharp nail), put your foot in a bucket of very hot water (the venom is de-activated by heat) and take a couple of painkillers. Sting relief spray (such as Wasp-eze) can also help.

JELLYFISH
Occasionally encountered on onshore days during the summer, jellyfish can sting exposed areas such as hands and feet, but your wetsuit will protect the rest of you.

SUNBURN
Even in Britain intense summer sunshine can cause sunburn and increase your risk of getting skin cancer. Be smart – use a waterproof sunblock.

RIP CURRENTS
Water pushed towards a beach by the action of waves flows back out to sea as a rip current. Rips can usually be identified from the shore as channels of deeper water (often between sandbars) where the waves aren't breaking: the surface of the water is usually rippled or choppy, and may be discoloured by suspended sand. A strong rip current can quickly drag you out to sea. If you get caught in a rip, don't try to paddle back to shore against the current, paddle across it to wherever the waves are breaking. Rip currents are often only 10 or 20 yards wide, so you can usually escape their clutches quite easily. Never leave your board: it's your life raft.

RIP CURRENTS

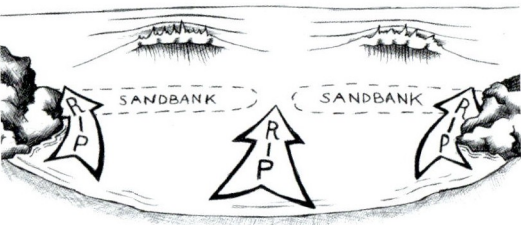

ANDREW CHISHOLM

A SPECTACULAR WIPE OUT AT SHIPSTERNS BLUFF.

BASICS

GETTING STARTED

Bodyboarding is a challenging sport to learn. It's physically demanding, often frustrating, and you need an incredible amount of patience. But ask any good bodyboarder why he or she does it and you'll get the same reply: because it's the best sport in the world. Bodyboarding can be exhilarating or relaxing, fast or slow, wild or controlled…whatever you want really, because how you ride your board is up to you.

If you want to learn to bodyboard, you need to be fit and you must be a good swimmer. Good eyesight is also important – if you normally wear contact lenses then wear them in the water.

Just as beginner skiers spend their first days on the slopes at a ski school, so beginner bodyboarders should spend their first days on the beach at a bodyboard school. Being taught the correct techniques by a properly-qualified instructor will save you hours of frustration. Lessons aren't expensive and they're good fun. Most importantly, it's vital that you learn about safety in the water: the ocean is a dangerous place to play if you don't know what you're doing. Check Robbarber.com for further info.

A FUN LOOKING TENERIFE REEF BREAK.

A FEW GROUND RULES

As well as the basic techniques of bodyboarding a school will teach you, you'll also come across a number of important ground rules, which apply to all surfers:
• DON'T bodyboard alone. It's always safer to surf with a mate or two…and a lot more fun.
• DON'T drop in. Recreational bodyboarding is a sport without hard-and-fast rules but there is one fundamental law: the surfer nearest the curl of the wave has right-of-way. Always.
• DON'T bodyboard straight after a meal, or after drinking alcohol.
• DON'T bail your board when paddling out through waves if you can possibly help it. There may be someone right behind you and they won't appreciate getting a board in the face.

Once you've had a few lessons at a bodyboarding school, learnt about water safety and got the right equipment, then you can get out there and learn at your own pace. Here are a few things you should do before hitting the water…
• DO spend a few minutes checking the conditions. Are there any rips or rocks? How frequent are the sets? Where are the other surfers and bodyboarders getting in and out of the water? If there aren't any other bodyboarders, there's probably a good reason. Maybe the waves are bigger than they look, in which case you'd be wise to try another more sheltered spot.
• DO check your equipment. Check that your leash is free of nicks or kinks. Wax the deck of your board so it's nice and grippy all over.
• DO something to warm up your muscles. Cold, stiff muscles and ligaments can easily be wrenched by a wipeout. You can avoid this by warming up or spending five minutes jogging (park further from the beach!).
• DO observe warning flags and restricted-area flags. These are used for safety purposes by lifeguards at most of the main surfing beaches from May to September.

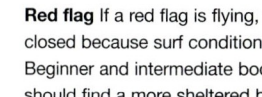 **Red flag** If a red flag is flying, the beach is closed because surf conditions are unsafe. Beginner and intermediate bodyboarders should find a more sheltered beach elsewhere. Experienced boogers who paddle out when a red flag is flying do so at their own risk…

 Black and white flag A zone with black-and-white chequered flags is a lifeguard-supervised area for beginner surfers and experienced bodyboarders. These areas sometimes get pretty crowded, with boards flying around all over the place, so keep your wits about you.

 **Red and yellow flag** A zone with yellow-and-red flags is an area for swimmers (and bodyboarders) only – enjoy the surfer-free peaks!

BASICS

SWELL PREDICTION

HOW TO FIGURE OUT WHEN THE SURF'S GOING TO PUMP

If you live by the coast (or have a boss who'll give you time off whenever you want it!) then you won't have to worry so much about predicting when the next swell's arriving. For the other 99.9 percent.... trying to forecast when the next swell will arrive is an integral part of being a bodyboarder. Especially if you only get to the coast at the weekend. Until recent times surfers were totally dependent on the BBC's long-range weather forecasts - but these days you can get an incredibly accurate surf prediction with a couple of clicks.

360mag.co.uk is a great place to start, and you'll find lots of useful pointers that will tell you when and where the surf will arrive. Although modern charts and services tend to be pretty idiot proof, it's still useful to know how surf is formed, so we run through it below. Learn the basics and then check out the charts for a change: it's quite rewarding!

So, you've clicked onto the site and you have weather a chart in front of you…what the hell does it all mean?

Isobars are the lines on a weather map. They actually represent 'contours' of atmospheric pressure. The important thing to know about isobars is that winds blow roughly parallel to them, and the closer the isobar, the stronger the wind.

Low pressure systems (depressions) are the swirling storm systems that generate most swells as they track across the ocean. The strong winds associated with lows rotate in an anti-clockwise direction. High pressure systems ('anti-cyclones') bring dry sunny weather and light winds, so they usually don't generate much swell. Winds rotate around highs in a clockwise direction.

Three factors determine the size and type of surf generated by a low pressure system: the wind-speed out at sea where the swell is being formed; how long the wind blows for and the fetch (the distance of open ocean that the wind blows across). Big clean swells are generated by strong winds blowing across a long fetch, preferably hundreds of miles away from where the swell arrives. Gentle breezes that blow short distance will only produce small choppy waves.

As waves travel across long distances they run together and organise themselves, eventually arriving in perfect lines - with regular sets of bigger waves. These sets usually contain four to six waves. Ocean swells generally move at 20 to 25 mph, so a swell generated by a low in the mid Atlantic will typically take three or four days to arrive on our shores.

QUICK TIP
Check out a number of different surf forecasting sites and average out the results. Remember their forecasts are only really an educated guess based on readings from open ocean buoys, so the best way to check the waves is to take an 'eye ball' check. You may find that you're pleasantly surprised... And there's no one else out!

CHECK OUT THE DIAGRAMS

Chart A shows a deep low pressure system in the mid-Atlantic. The blue arrow shows the area where swell is being generated, and the direction it's travelling in. This low will produce a big southwest swell, heading straight for Devon, Cornwall, Wales and southwest Ireland. It should also provide waves for the Channel Islands and the south coast. If the area of high pressure centred over Britain stayed put for a few days, the result would be offshore winds in most areas giving classic surfing conditions.

A

Chart B shows an ideal weather map for Scotland and the East Coast, with a storm centred over Scandinavia. The strong northerly airflow coming down from the Arctic will generate a powerful swell which will arrive a couple of days later; by that time the next low will be approaching from the west, bringing southwest winds – bang offshore!

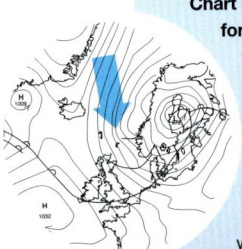

B

Reading the charts may seem difficult at first, but with a bit of perseverance you'll soon reap the rewards. By learning about weather charts you can begin to predict when a new swell will hit, how big it'll be, and be ready on the beach when it arrives.

When open-ocean swells move into shallower water they decelerate, 'feel' the seabed, and eventually break as waves. The manner in which waves break depends largely on the configuration of the seabed.

BEACHBREAKS

Beachbreaks – such as Fistral Beach in Cornwall – are the best place for beginners to learn to bodyboard as the waves tend to be slower and they break over sand. The peaks at a beachbreak will move around from one week to another as the sandbars below shift with the currents.

POINTBREAKS

Pointbreaks – like Lynmouth in Devon – are rocky headlands around which waves peel (either to the left or right). Good pointbreaks provide long, racy waves which 'wall up' as you ride along them. They're not suitable for beginners (because of rocks and rip currents), but are fine for competent intermediates.

REEFBREAKS

Reefbreaks – like Porthleven in Cornwall – are the most demanding breaks of all, and should only be tackled by advanced bodyboarders. These are spots where waves break straight onto shallow ledges of rock. If conditions are perfect, a reefbreak will sometimes provide barrelling waves as the lip of the breaking wave pitches and throws out to form a tube.

WEDGES

A wedge wave is formed by an incoming wave and a refraction wave (or bounce) connecting up to produce a wave that looks like a moving corner. As the wave effectively has the power of two waves together it offers twice the power and twice the speed of a normal wave if you catch it correctly. But beware, it is also twice as heavy if it breaks on your head! Coupled with a shorebreak, this is a bodyboarder's favourite type of wave.

LOOK CLOSELY AND YOU CAN SEE ONE OF THE LOCALS JUST CRUISING BELOW THE SURFACE.

A SOUTH CORNWALL SECRET SPOT.

A few of the very best pointbreaks and reefbreaks in Britain and Ireland are referred to in surfing lore as 'secret spots'. These are places the local surfers and bodyboarders don't want overrun by other wave riders. For that reason we've not included such spots in this publication. If you're a good enough bodyboarder with a respectful attitude then you'll find them if you look for them. As the old surfing adage goes: "Seek and ye shall find!"

BASICS

WAVES

MICKEY SMITH

Ocean waves are some of the most complicated phenomena on earth. However, you don't need to become an oceanographer to understand the basics of how they're formed, and how they break.

Waves come in all shapes and sizes, but the majority of them are produced the same way: by winds blowing across the oceans and creating swells. (The exceptions are tsunamis which are caused by submarine earthquakes, and tidal waves such as the Severn Bore.)

The best type of swells for surfing are groundswells, which are generated many hundreds of miles away by winds revolving around distant low pressure systems.

Classic surfing conditions occur when a solid groundswell combines with an offshore wind – lines of waves can be seen stacked up way out to sea, and the waves themselves are smooth and a joy to ride.

Well-organised groundswells are made up of 'trains' of waves, some of which are slightly out of synch with the others. When the crests of two wave trains synchronise, the result is a group of larger waves called a 'set'. Experienced surfers sit and wait for these sets, which arrive at regular intervals, because they're always the biggest and the best waves.

When a low pressure system passes close to the shore it brings stormy, wet weather and a different type of swell called a windswell. Windswell waves can be just as big as groundswell waves but they're choppy, disorganised, and tend to back-off a lot... in other words they're rarely as much fun to ride.

DAY BREAK AIR REVERSE.

LET'S GET STARTED

CONTENTS

8 BASICS
- 8 Waves
- 10 Swell predition
- 11 Getting started
- 12 Hazards
- 14 Emergencies
- 17 Equipment
- 18 Boards
- 22 Quick Tips
- 24 Duck Diving, Paddling
- 25 Trimming, Bottom turns

26 INTERMEDIATE
- 26 Cut backs
- 27 Off the rocks
- 28 Forwards spins
- 29 Reverse spin
- 30 Cut back to forward spin
- 31 Air roll
- 32 Reverse floater

34 ADVANCED
- 34 Tube riding
- 36 Invert air
- 37 Cut back reverse
- 38 Air reverse
- 39 Air forward
- 40 Gyroll
- 41 Front Flip
- 42 Air Roll
- 43 Back Flip

44 DROP KNEE
- 44 Getting up
- 45 Drop knee floaters
- 46 Drop knee cuttie
- 47 Drop knee tube
- 48 Drop Knee Air

50 EXTRA TIPS
- Winter motivaton

52 LOCATIONS (UK AND IRELAND)
- 53 Ireland
- 54 North cornwall
- 54 South cornwall
- 54 North devon
- 54 South devon
- 56 Wales
- 56 Channel islands
- 58 North east
- 59 Soctland
- 60 South coast

62 LOCATIONS (INTERNATIONAL)

65 GLOSSARY

CONTENTS

ALEX ORMEROD

Publishing Director Mike Searle **Joint Publisher** Louise Searle **Editor** Rob Barber **Advertising Manager** Louise Searle **Design** David Alcock **Photography** Mike Searle, Mickey Smith, Will Bailey, Tim Jones, Jacob Cockle, Alex Williams, EstPix, Gary Knights, Dave Ferguson, Alex Ormerod **Contributors** Jacob Cockle, Ali Daniels, Joe Franklin, Ryan Phelps **Repro** Picture House Ltd, St Austell **Printed by** Advent Colour, Andover

Unsolicited contributions are welcome but must be accompanied by a stamped addressed envelope. While all care will be taken to ensure their safety, the publishers cannot accept responsibility for any loss or damage caused to manuscripts, artwork and photographs, or for their return. All material in ThreeSixty is copyright and reproduction without asking is a big no-no! While every care is taken in compiling ThreeSixty the publishers assume no responsibility for any affect arising from any omissions or errors. The views of the authors are not necessarily those of the publishers. © Orca Publications Ltd 2010

Published by Orca Publications Ltd, Berry Road Studios, Berry Road, Newquay, Cornwall TR7 1AT.
Tel 01637 878074 **Fax** 01637 850226 **e-mail:** info@orcasurf.co.uk
Website: www.orcasurf.co.uk

ON THE COVER: RYAN 'MAD DOG' MATTICK PLUMBS THROUGH A TASTY IRISH BARREL. PHOTO: MICKEY SMITH

ALL PHOTOS BY MIKE SEARLE UNLESS OTHERWISE STATED. SHOT ON LOCATION IN TENERIFE.

INTRO

WELCOME

THE EPITOME OF BODYBOARDING FUN; SHOREBREAK BARRELS. KIA ROBERTS ENJOYING HIMSELF IN SOUTH CORNWALL.

Welcome to the ThreeSixty Bodyboard Manual in association with Rob Barber's Bodyboarding School!

This is the fourth edition of our guide to all things bodyboarding.

Bodyboarding has moved on a long way since July 7th 1971 when Tom Morey fashioned the first bodyboard using whatever he had kicking about: an electric carving knife, a clothes iron, some packing foam and some newspaper. He took it out for a few sessions, and the 'Boogie Board' (as it was branded back then) was born.

Things have moved on a bit since those days, and there is now a multi million pound industry behind the sport and a legitimate world tour with professional riders going balls to the wall in some of the most hectic wave conditions on the planet. International stars like Ronaldo and Cameron Diaz can be seen in celebrity magazines riding bodyboards. The sport is accessible to all, opening up wave riding to the masses at one end of the spectrum and offering the most extreme wave riding vehicle at the other. The bodyboard is revered as one of the most functional bits of kit in the world's most lurching, heavy, and once thought "unrideable" reefs.

Learning to bodyboard is a healthy addiction that will consume you, and learning the right way from the start will enrich your experience, increase your enjoyment and sky rocket your progression.

I've been bodyboarding for longer than I care to mention, I've competed for and coached the national team, been national champion, owned Britain's premiere bodyboarding school for the last 15 years and I still fall over my own fins if I'm not paying attention! I hope that my experiences will help ease you through every stage of your riding, and get you through those tricky phases that can have you cursing the day you ever picked up a bodyboard!

Australian born drop knee specialist, top UK coach and past national drop knee champion Aidan Salmon also unravels some of the secrets of drop knee riding. Plus we thank some of our top international friends including world champ's Jeff Hubbard and Ben Player for their contribution to the manual – with their inspirational and flawless bodyboarding technique caught by our photographers and unravelled for you.

Well – if you're just starting out then prepare to be amazed by the thrill of harnessing the unrelenting power of ocean waves, astounded by the beauty of nature and addicted to a new lifestyle – from the first time the salty foam caresses your skin and washes through your sinuses! The basics of bodyboarding are easily learnt, but to master the intricacies of wave riding takes a life time...

If you've already got a few years under your belt then hopefully this edition of the manual will help you get a few more moves dialled, and unlock some of the secrets that will take your riding up a notch...

Whatever your standard: remember that the best bodyboarder in the water is the one having the most fun!

Rob Barber, Editor

ThreeSixty
BODYBOARD MAGAZINE

www.threesixtymag.co.uk

THE BIBLE OF BRITISH BODYBOARDING SINCE '92

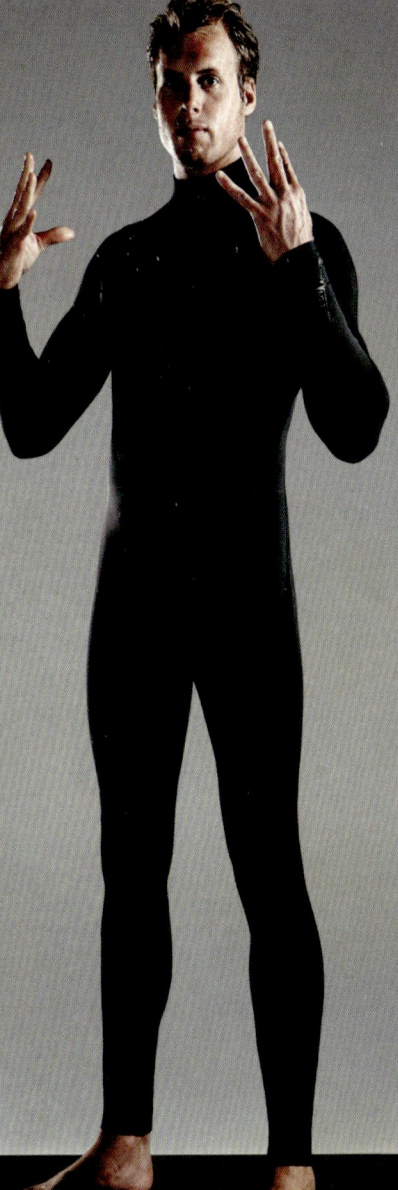

 NAKED F3... NO DOUBT YOU HAVE HEARD ABOUT OUR NAKED F3 NEOPRENE, A TRADEMARK OF AGENT EIGHTEEN. IMAGINE THE FEELING OF ORGANIC NAKEDNESS WHILST FLYING THROUGH THE AIR? BEAUTIFUL. CHECK ✓

 FIREFLEX... FEEL AN INVISIBLE, INTERNAL BODY SUIT WHILST RADIATING PURE WARMTH AND ABSOLUTE FLEX? CHECK ✓

 CONTOUR FIT... THE FIT OF A WELL MEASURED, TAILORED SUIT. A CUT SO FINE AND BALANCED YOU LITERALLY SLICE THROUGH GRAVITY, SURELY NOT? ACTUALLY, YES. ONLY WITH AGENT EIGHTEEN.

 3D INK... PUT SIMPLY, OUR 3D INK CHEST BADGES JUST LOOK WAY COOLER AND DONT RUB OR FADE, EVER. CHECK ✓

 DIAMOND FLEX PADS... THE DIAMOND FINISH IN ALL OUR SUITS. NO BLOOD. CHECK ✓

 CRITICALLY TAPED SEAMS... WE CALL THIS OUR 'ILLUSIVE' FEATURE, AS IT DOESNT EVEN FEEL LIKE THERE ARE 'SEAMS'. CHECK ✓

 DRAINAGE SYSTEM - WE NOT HOLDING YOU BACK KIDS! THIS EXCLUSIVE FEATURE IN ALL CHEST ZIP SUITS WILL ELIMINATE ANY EXTRA WEIGHT YOU MIGHT BE CARRYING. CLEARLY ALLOWING FOR ULTIMATE SPEED, COMFORT AND ESSENTIALLY YOUR PERFORMANCE. PURE PERFORMANCE. CHECK ✓

 THE ALL NEW AGENT EIGHTEEN DISTRIBUTED EXCLUSIVELY BY WE-TRADING - EUROPE - USA - STH AFRICA - WWW.WE-TRADING.COM - CHECK ✓